PREACHING AT THE PARISH COMMUNION

I

ON THE GOSPELS

D. W. Cleverley Ford

LONDON
A. R. MOWBRAY & CO LTD

© A. R. Mowbray & Co Ltd 1967

*Printed in Great Britain by
Alden & Mowbray Ltd, at the Alden Press, Oxford*

SBN 264 655 257

*First published in 1967
Third impression 1968*

PREFACE

This book has been written in response to an invitation from the publishing department of Messrs. A. R. Mowbray and Company. I am indebted to William Purcell, Residentiary Canon of Worcester, for reading the original typescript, and giving his valuable advice, and to Mrs. J. Hodgson for preparing the typed copy from my manuscript. Use has been made of the New English Bible, New Testament, copyright 1961, by permission of Oxford and Cambridge University Presses.

Kensington 1966 *D. W. Cleverley Ford*

CONTENTS

Introduction　　Sermon bonework　　*Page* 1

Sermon outlines based on the Gospels in the Book of Common Prayer:

ADVENT 1	What has God's house become?	7
ADVENT 2	The unexpected	8
ADVENT 3	Expectancy	10
ADVENT 4	God needs roads	14
CHRISTMAS EVE	Christ in the dark	15
CHRISTMAS DAY	Christ enters the real world	18
EPIPHANY 1	Our justification	21
EPIPHANY 2	Gaiety	25
EPIPHANY 3	No barriers	29
EPIPHANY 4	Christ's strange authority	31
EPIPHANY 5	Masterly inactivity	35
EPIPHANY 6	Deceivers	36
SEPTUAGESIMA	Life and logic	38
SEXAGESIMA	How to listen	40
QUINQUAGESIMA	A broken thing	42
LENT 1	The use of power	43
LENT 2	Love through rules	46
LENT 3	The peril of emptiness	49
LENT 4	God recognizes ordinary things	53
LENT 5	In God's time	54
PALM SUNDAY	A woman of society	57
GOOD FRIDAY	An advertisement	61
EASTER DAY	The new dimension	64
EASTER 1	Life of a different quality	67
EASTER 2	The pattern	70
EASTER 3	New birth	72
EASTER 4	The interpreter	73
EASTER 5	Buoyancy	74
SUNDAY AFTER ASCENSION DAY	Forewarning	77

WHITSUNDAY	The Church discloses the Spirit	*Page*	78
TRINITY SUNDAY	New life		80
TRINITY 1	Hell		82
TRINITY 2	What is the Kingdom of God like?		85
TRINITY 3	Self-defence		87
TRINITY 4	Blind guides		88
TRINITY 5	Deep water		89
TRINITY 6	About anger		91
TRINITY 7	Man's wealth needs Christ		93
TRINITY 8	The way of entry		96
TRINITY 9	Money		100
TRINITY 10	Recognition		101
TRINITY 11	Look up, not down		103
TRINITY 12	Hearing and speaking		104
TRINITY 13	My neighbour		105
TRINITY 14	Men afar off		107
TRINITY 15	Anxiety		109
TRINITY 16	The barrier of bereavement		111
TRINITY 17	Exclusiveness excluded		112
TRINITY 18	A sharp tongue		114
TRINITY 19	A passenger		115
TRINITY 20	Not bothering		117
TRINITY 21	Thy son liveth		118
TRINITY 22	Ethics		119
TRINITY 23	The sacred and the secular		121
TRINITY 24	Disease and death		122
TRINITY 25	Nothing lost		123

INTRODUCTION

Sermon bonework

This book is meant to be a manual for busy clergy. It must not be judged on its literary merits, or lack of such merits. Nor must it be weighed on account of its scholarship, or lack of scholarship. Other writings of mine have paid attention to both these important aspects of pulpit work. In the present book, the aim is to try and show the bonework of some sermons, so as to indicate how such bonework may be constructed, and what it is that gets clothed to form the finished sermon.

First of all, bonework there must be. A body will not stand up without bones, nor will a sermon. It is true, the bones must not protrude overmuch, though bonework in a face can make it handsome. Bones, however, there must be. And after the sermon has been delivered by the preacher, little of it will be remembered by the time the hearers have reached home (except, perhaps, some telling illustration), unless it has a shape, made possible by bonework. As bonework outlasts the flesh in a body, so it does in a sermon.

Secondly, the bonework must fit together. There is a unity about every skeleton. The arm and leg bones connect up with the spine. So there must be a unity about a sermon. Another way of expressing this same necessity is to say that a sermon must have one aim, one theme, one main thought. There may be two, three or four points in the sermon, but they must all belong to the one theme. They must not be separate. There cannot be separate bone structures in one body. The rule is, one skeleton, one body. One theme with subpoints, one sermon.

These are the two main essentials about preparing a sermon—Theme and Shape. And they are essential, not because this is pulpit orthodoxy, but because the sermon has to be listened to, and not absorbed by reading, and it can only be received by the mind through the ears if it possesses shape made possible by a unified bonework.

The sermon also needs an aim. The preacher may decide, for example, that the theme of the Gospel for Advent Sunday is 'Christ as the judge of the use men make of God's house!' But he also has to decide why he is going to present that theme to *his* congregation. He has to decide this because preaching is not conveying information. That is lecturing. In preaching, he is seeking to move the will of his hearers, by kindling the imagination, so as to evoke a response to God's word in practice. He must, of course, have responded himself to that word. Then his aim will be in no doubt. On Advent Sunday, if he develops the theme mentioned, it will be in order to purge his own church of unworthy usages, so that it may become a true house of prayer. His aim will be to make God's house a house of prayer. All this will be seen to be implicit in the text, because it has been drawn out of the text. The text is, 'It is written, My house shall be called the house of prayer; but ye have made it a den of thieves.' They constitute the closing words of the Gospel for Advent Sunday.

A great secret in being able to set up the bonework at the start is developing the ability to select a verse from the Gospel which both sums up the theme of the lection and allows of development. One of the simplest ways of doing this is to look for a picture word somewhere in the narrative which embraces the theme. On Advent 4 the picture word selected could be 'Way' or 'Road.' This, then, forms the backbone of the sermon skeleton. On Good Friday, it could be 'Advertisement,' and this, again, holds the bonework of the sermon together. Moreover, these picture words enable the sermon to be presented pictorially, instead of in the form of abstraction, and this, again, is a basic necessity, if the sermon is to be received.

It will be seen that, for the most part, the sermon outlines in this collection begin with a text. This is not essential. The text can be introduced later in the sermon, or at the end, but obviously, a sermon on the Gospel for the day will be more easily remembered if it is recognized as the exposition of a text.

Most of the sermon outlines here also have an Introduction, Three points, and a Conclusion. The number of the points is not important, though the number three, somehow, has a certain naturalness about it. There must, however, be a 'lead-in' or introduction of some kind, and there must be a conclusion or application. Notice that neither introduction nor conclusion are laboured. And notice that quite often, though not always, the introduction begins where the people are, that is to say, it keys into their interests. A sermon must lead the hearers to a point at which they have not yet arrived. It must, therefore, begin where they are, and not where the preacher hopes they will be, when he has finished his sermon.

In a few cases in this book the sermons have been written out in full. This has been done intentionally, so that the finished product may be seen. It will be noticed that there is still a recognizable shape, and the aim is detectable in the introduction, and the conclusion or application. The sentences will be seen to be short, straightforward and with a minimum of subordinate clauses. The words selected are, for the most part, simple English words.

Some surprise may be experienced that local and personal references are left standing in this book. This, again, has been done on purpose. A sermon must arise out of, and belong to, a concrete situation. All preaching must be existential in the sense that it must belong to experience, the preacher's, and the hearers'. It cannot, therefore, consist of general and universal truths. All sermons which are proper sermons must date badly. If not, they are bad sermons. Fear of involving preaching in time and space makes for Docetism. The word has to become flesh in the pulpit, and flesh is weak, fallible and quick to decay. The word of God, however, must become flesh, and not a fossil. Only flesh is warm. Not many people will take to fossils.

Sermons have to be preached. They must not be read in the pulpit, unless, of course, the preacher is John Henry

Newman. The television age has taught people by viewing to expect direct confrontation. The speaker must look straight into the camera, and into the eye of the viewers. There is little doubt that a modern television-conditioned congregation will write off a preacher who is tied to his manuscript. So the sermon has to be in a form that makes it memorable for the preacher. Hence the importance, again, of bonework. If he cannot remember his sermon, can he expect his hearers to do so?

To achieve this, the present writer carries out the following plan, week by week.

1. Read the Gospel and decide what is the main theme of the scripture passage, and which text embodies that theme. This settles the text.

2. Then decide for what purpose the theme is going to be handled for the congregation. This settles the aim.

3. Set up the skeleton, or bonework of the sermon; that is, provide an Introduction, Two or Three points, and a Conclusion. All are held together by the one aim and theme.

4. Next, write out the whole sermon, word for word, using the skeleton. That is to say, cover the bonework with flesh, verbal flesh, as attractive as possible to the likes of the hearers.

5. The fifth task is to reduce the sermon manuscript to a number of headings on a postcard. It will be shorter than the original bonework, but will obviously correspond with it.

6. Read the sermon manuscript aloud in the study the day before preaching it, and then speak it out in the study, using only the postcard with its headings.

7. Finally, leave both manuscript and postcard headings at home, and go and preach directly to the people.

Obviously, this preparation must extend over some days prior to the preaching, and it is well to begin early in each week. The beginner may not be able to accomplish all seven of these points. He will probably be wise, however, to make sure of the first four in his practice. And every preacher will have occasions when he considers it wise to take his manuscript into the pulpit. Even so, he must *preach* from it, and not *read* from it. The paramount necessity is to know the sermon thoroughly, so that attention can be given to delivery. Delivery, however, is another subject beyond the scope of this book, and introduction, which is mainly concerned with sermon bonework.

It cannot be stressed too much that each preacher must develop his own method. No two persons are alike, no two preachers, and no two preachers' methods. But method there must be, and in that method, attention to the unifying theme and bonework of the sermon. And in all this, it is taken for granted that the first preparation of a sermon takes place on the knees, close to the presence of God; and, over all that is done in study and pulpit, there extends the urgent sense of mission. The preacher must be bent on reaching Christ's sheep that are scattered abroad, otherwise he will not be preaching.

ADVENT 1

What has God's house become?

St. Matthew 21. 13 *'My house shall be called the house of prayer; but ye have made it a den of thieves.'*

INTRODUCTION

He seemed so innocuous, riding there upon an ass into Jerusalem. His mount and his demeanour recalled the words, 'Tell ye the daughter of Zion, Behold, thy King cometh unto thee, meek, and sitting upon an ass, and a colt the foal of an ass.' And his supporters were humble enough, spreading their garments in the way, and cutting down branches from the trees, and strawing them in the way. No need to fear this motley crowd, or its modest captain! But when this leader arrived in the capital city, he became an energetic judge. He overthrew the tables of the money-changers in the temple, and labelled it 'a den of thieves.'

There is nothing frightening about the *manner* in which Christ comes to either man or city. There is nothing frightening about his advent, to be celebrated in only a few weeks' time. What can be more meek than a baby in a manger? But Christ is the judge. He judges us by his presence. He will label us for what we are. He will label our church for what it is. What have we made our church?

1. *A house or a home*

A beautiful house with everything in its place just like a showroom in a furniture store? A home is a very different thing from a house. A home is concerned with furniture only so far as it affects people. There is warmth, affection and refreshment in a home. Have we made our church a home to the community in which it is set, or is it merely a house containing ecclesiastical furniture?

2. *An efficient social machine*

Efficiency is necessary in a church. The social needs of the community must be met by the church as far as is possible.

But social ends relentlessly pursued turn the church into a machine, and a machine is soulless.

3. *How will our church be labelled*

A club for the religiously-minded, or for those of a particular religious outlook. This is unhealthy. A church should be outward looking, outreaching. It must have a sense of mission.

How do people label our church? More important, how does Christ label it? We must think of our own local church. It is easy to label the church in the next parish, or the Church of England as a whole. We do this to dodge the judgement on ourselves. We are afraid of that label Christ might affix on the door of our building.

CONCLUSION

What should a church be, first and foremost? A house of prayer. A place where belief in God turns into communion with God, and communion with God turns into action for people. Christ would probably not label our church a den of thieves, but would he call it a house of prayer? A place not where we take *from* our fellowmen, but where we learn what we may *give* our fellowmen.

ADVENT 2

The unexpected

> St. Luke 21. 25 *'And there shall be signs in the sun, and in the moon, and in the stars; and upon the earth distress of nations....'*

INTRODUCTION

We can recognize our own times in this. Anxiety is widespread. Everywhere men are afraid of what is coming on the earth. But what does today's Gospel say? 'When these things begin to come to pass, then look up, and lift up your heads; for your redemption draweth nigh.' What are the lessons?

1. *Hard times*

When outward circumstances are at their most frightening, that is the time to expect God to act. A Christian who believes this, and in consequence 'lifts up his head' when times are hard, will stand out like a beacon light in a community.

2. *Self-despair*

When a man is brought to the end of himself, when he is conscious that his own resources have failed, when his own weakness stares him in the face, then he may know that he is not far from the Kingdom of God. Christ came to be born in a stable, where there was apparently nothing worthy of making him a suitable cradle. When a man despairs of himself, that is the time for him to hope in God.

3. *Christ most often appears as the unexpected Christ*

He was not expected in a stable. He was not expected in Nazareth. He was not expected in the storm-tossed sea of Galilee. He was not expected among the publicans and sinners. He was not expected to be seen on a cross. He was not expected to be seen alive in the garden where he was buried. We must never think we can 'get the measure' of Christ. He will always do above all we ask or think.

CONCLUSION

So today's Gospel is a challenge to our (1) gloominess, (2) self-sufficiency, (3) rationalism. We are confronted with the great God, the God who is never brought to an end of himself, by what happens on the earth, or in any human heart. To trust in this God is to know the secret of never being defeated in spirit by whatever happens. It is to this buoyancy Advent stirs the whole Church. It should rise up with expectancy, whatever the circumstances. Bad signs are hopeful signs to Christian eyes. Do we possess these eyes?

ADVENT 3

Expectancy

> St. Matthew 11. 3 (NEB) *'Are you the one who is to come, or are we to expect some other?'*

INTRODUCTION

Some time ago I read of a young clergyman who was bewailing the poverty of his ministry. There seemed so little response to his labours, and in particular to his preaching, that he was thoroughly disheartened. And then one day coming across another minister whose work had prospered mightily, he opened up his heart, laying bare for the other to see the nakedness of his heart. 'Nothing ever happens in my ministry,' he confessed, 'no stirring in the pews, no sign of any spiritual elevation.' 'But,' said the older counsellor, 'surely you do not expect results every time you preach?' 'Well, no,' said the young man, 'as a matter of fact I don't.' And swiftly and sharply there came back the reply, 'That is the chief reason why you do not get any.'

All of us, not only preachers, have to learn very quickly the importance of expectancy in the spiritual life. Without it we receive very little. With it the most extraordinary results are possible. The truth has been expressed like this, 'attempt great things *for* God, expect great things *from* God.' And the same attitude of expectancy lies behind these words of Jesus, 'Whatsoever things ye shall ask in prayer, believing, ye shall receive.' More than many of us dare to believe it is our own expectancy, or lack of it, that governs what comes to us in life.

Now, on this third Sunday in Advent, we think of two men approaching Jesus with a question. Ostensibly, it was the question of John the Baptist incarcerated in Fort Machaerus for daring to criticize the marriage of Herod Antipas, the question of a man whose faith, by reason of what had happened to him, had burned low. Perhaps it was the question of the two men themselves. Whoever it was, it was an important question. It still is an important question. What they asked of Jesus was, 'Are you the one who is to come, or are we to expect some other?'

1. *John's disciples possessed expectancy*

The first fact you will notice is that these men were expecting someone. 'Are you the one who is to come, or are we to expect some other?' And that, you see, was the great advantage of the Jewish people: for hundreds of years they had been schooled to expect a Messiah, or at least a Messianic Kingdom. But we so often these days expect nothing. There are tens of thousands of people who are satisfied with life, satisfied with its material resources, satisfied with its multifarious pleasures, more and more of which have now come within the range of all. Or, if they reckon that there is room for a great many improvements in life, they assume that man has the power within himself to shape this satisfactory future, and only time is needed for the desirable to be realized.

To all of these, the Advent question, 'Are you the one who is to come, or are we to expect some other?' makes no sense. Being without wants they are without the possibility of expectancy, and being without expectancy, they have only the slenderest possibilities of developing any kind of spiritual vigour.

2. *A feeble expectancy of Jesus*

A second fact you note about this question is that it was doubtfully asked. Here were two people to whom life had not given all that they might desire. Perhaps theirs was a very narrow lot. Perhaps they felt in themselves they had the capacity for far more than their opportunities afforded, and they may have been right. In all probability they looked out on a world in which innocent men were often crushed by the powerful, where greed often achieved its purpose, where suspicion allowed no room even for the existence of the honourable. And in their hearts there burned still the passion for an upright world, a world where goodness was rewarded, and it paid to tell the truth.

They found it hard to believe, however, that Jesus could be

the one to bring in that kind of world. True, he had the goodness in himself; true, thousands of men were aware of his subtle attraction, but could a man who obviously refused to climb to the seats of worldly power ever accomplish anything on a world scale? If Jesus would not challenge Caesar, how could there ever be anyone ruling the world but Caesar? So these men ask their doubtful question, 'Are you the one who is to come, or are we to expect some other?'

And that could be any one of us speaking today. A man two thousand years ago in a backward province of the old Roman Empire, what can he do to change the trickery, graft, sordidness and sheer selfishness that festers everywhere just below the level of outward respectability? Does not the very antiquity of the man from Nazareth smother any expectancy we might have of him as our leader to a better world? 'Are you the one who is to come, or are we to expect some other?'

3. *Jesus' answer concerning himself*

But Jesus answered this question himself. Not, however, with a direct 'Yes' or 'No.' Quite often God does not answer us with a direct 'Yes' or 'No.' Jesus said, 'If you look around you, you will see evidence that I *am* the one who is to come.' Not proof, but evidence. Wherever God is present you will see extraordinary events taking place. You may call them miracles if you like, they are certainly wonderful works, 'the blind receive their sight, the lame walk, and the lepers are clean, the deaf hear, the dead are raised up, the poor are hearing the good news.' And that last phrase tacked on at the end puzzles us most of all. 'The poor are hearing the good news.' But that is as much evidence of the presence of God as a lame man walking. Normally, poor men do not receive an announcement about God. They only receive an announcement about money and clothes and food, and is it any wonder? This is the remarkable fact about the Christian Gospel. It has lifted the poor man up.

No, there is no proof that Jesus is the one on whom we should fasten our expectancy, no proof which will relieve us of the burden of making a decision, but there is everything to urge us to make a decision. The work of Christ provokes us to scorn or ridicule or sheer disbelief—'The blind recover their sight, the lame walk, the lepers are clean . . .' or they provoke us to acceptance and wonder and faith. So Jesus ended his message to the two inquirers on behalf of John—'And happy is the man who does not find me a stumbling block.'

APPLICATION

What do we make of Christ? Some do not make anything of him, because they are too busy with things. Others do not make anything of him because they only see him as a historical figure belonging to a past age. But wherever in our groping, stumbling, sin-stained, insensitive society, for every member of which, be it remembered, there lies the unavoidable prospect of the grave and nothingness, wherever we detect evidence of buoyancy, vision, uprightness and hope, a hope no death can kill, then we are bound to ask if it is not true, after all, that in the world, the Christ *is* present, the risen Christ, the contemporary Christ, the Christ who works miracles. That is the provocation; to decide if Christ is not after all the one about whom all our deepest expectations should gather.

> Come, thou long-expected Jesus,
> Born to set thy people free;
> From our fears and sins release us;
> Let us find our rest in thee.
>
> C. WESLEY, 1746

And if we have decided, then the word of God for us today is this, expect great things from Christ. Not necessarily what you plan. Not necessarily what you ask, but what God wills, and his will is good. Do not be surprised if miracles happen. I am preaching to myself this morning, for I know the power of rationalism to kill expectancy. But we must look for miracles. It is largely because we twentieth-century men expect so little from Christ that we receive so little. In the spiritual life the key word is expectancy, the conditioning word is expectancy. We must expect great things from God. It is the Advent message, the Advent hope and the Advent consolation. God will do for us more than we ask or think, if we expect him to....

ADVENT 4

God needs roads

St. John 1. 23 *'Make straight the way of the Lord.'*

INTRODUCTION

At present, there is a great deal of dissatisfaction with Britain's roads. They are not counted as sufficient, or satisfactory, to carry the ever-increasing weight of Britain's road traffic. We sometimes wonder if our big cities will seize up altogether, unless something drastic is done about the roads.

We can understand how motor-cars need roads. It comes as something of a surprise that God should need roads. But the fact is, there will be no flow of spiritual traffic in our lives, or in the life of the church, unless there are adequate roads.

Of course God may break in unexpectedly into someone's life. He may cross a desert to do it. But what we are thinking about today is the regular life of professing Christians. Each one must keep the spiritual roads in his life straight, or he will have little contact with God, and God will have little effective contact with him.

1. *Spiritual roads*

What are some of the spiritual roads in our lives? I suggest worship, private prayer, the Holy Communion, Bible-reading, fellowship in active Christian work. Without these, it is not impossible, but it is unlikely, that God will come to human experience as a living reality.

2. Blocked roads

What are some of the reasons why our roads become blocked or crooked? I suggest inefficient planning of our week, so that Sunday is overcrowded with chores. Pride, which makes us unwilling to follow a simple rule of life. Unwillingness to mix with Church people.

3. Roadmaking

Roadmaking is a strenuous business. Advent is meant to be a strenuous time. We are called to force a way through the mountain of tasks that lie before us at this season of the year, and *make time and opportunity* for God to speak to us, in the secret recesses of our own souls.

CONCLUSION

Imagine a city where all the roads are blocked. No possibility of food deliveries! No possibility of the doctor calling! It would be a dead city. A man can be dead in the same way. So can a church. Therefore the call is, 'Make straight the way of the Lord.'

CHRISTMAS EVE

Christ in the dark

INTRODUCTION

I wonder if you were afraid of the dark when you were a child. I wonder if you had to have a light left burning by your bed, a night-light, or you would not go to sleep. Perhaps we smile over those childish fears. But does fear of the dark ever wholly leave us? After all, are not burglaries made in the dark? And in war bombs dropped in the dark? And does not the sick man on his bed of pain toss more terribly through the long hours of darkness? Yes, we fear the dark.

1. *Christ was born into the dark*

But now in the midst of this midnight service, the first Communion of Christmas, I am able to tell you that in the midst of the thing we fear, Christ was born. We do not know exactly the date. We do not even know the month. All the months of the year have been suggested. We do not even know for certain the year. It may have been 4 B.C. (odd as this sounds). One thing, however, we do know. He was born at night.

'There were shepherds abiding in the fields keeping watch over their flocks by night.' Christ was born in the dark.

Why are we afraid of the dark? Isn't it because we don't quite know *what* is out there, *who* is out there? There could be someone in hiding, watching, waiting, listening for us. I thought of that about six weeks ago when I made my way late at night along a deserted country lane, searching for a house.

And the future is dark. We don't know what is out there six months hence, or six years hence, waiting for us. Some illness, some setback. And the whole world seems dark at the moment, dark and foreboding.

But this is the word of God at this time. Out in the dark, whatever else there may be, out in the dark is Christ. He was born in the dark, cradled in the dark. Joseph had to lift a lantern so that Mary could see the features of her first-born child. And the shepherds had to make their way to a darkened Bethlehem.

> O little town of Bethlehem,
>   How still we see thee lie!
> Above thy deep and dreamless sleep
>   The silent stars go by:
> Yet in thy dark streets shineth
>   The everlasting Light;
> The hopes and fears of all the years
>   Are met in thee tonight.
>   BISHOP P. BROOKS

Yes, the dark holds terrors for us all, but Christmas Eve tells us the dark also holds Christ if we will only look and see.

2. *The darkness never quenches the Light which is Christ*

I remember when I was a boy of fourteen, being taken down on the day after Boxing Day to an old summer-house, by the side of a river, on a stretch of desolate marshland in Norfolk. The wind was howling from the north-east. The few bare willow trees acting as a windbreak around the enclosure were bent almost double. My host slept in the summer-house, and I was housed in a houseboat pulled up on the land. It seemed horribly dark when I crossed that little enclosure, picking my steps, to climb into the houseboat. There was no moon, no stars, only the howling wind and the lapping of the water. But when I lay in my bunk, the hurricane lamp turned out, through the porthole I saw a light in the darkness, perhaps a mile away, one tiny light. And it sent me to sleep. Perhaps it was the marshman's cottage, the only building near at all, but it comforted me. And when I awoke in the night, half afraid at the eerieness, I looked for the light, and there it was. The darkness had not quenched it. And it put my boyish mind at rest. I went to sleep till morning.

'The Light shines on in the dark, and the darkness has never quenched it.' So says the Gospel for today in the New English Bible Version. And that is how we are to think of Christ. He is a light in the dark that never goes out. A light in the dark which takes the terror from the dark. A light we need to fix our eyes upon whenever the clouds are gathering.

Canon Peter Green tells how when he was a schoolboy he asked another boy what it meant to be religious. 'Oh,' said the other, 'there are some things you mustn't do, like cheating, lying, swearing and listening to dirty talk.' Then suddenly his face changed. 'No, it is not,' he added, 'do you really want to know what religion is? Well, it's waking up in the middle of the night and remembering you belong to God, and turning over and going to sleep again happy because of it.'

'The Light shines on in the dark, and the darkness has never quenched it.'

APPLICATION

As you come forward in a few minutes to receive the sacred elements and to make your communion with the Eternal Spirit of God, and with one another, will you remember this? Christ came in the dark so that we should never wholly fear what is dark to us again. There *is* darkness in the world. Quite often there is darkness in the human heart. But we shall not be overwhelmed if we keep our eyes on the Light which is Christ. There is no Christless dark anywhere. He came to Bethlehem in the dark to show us this. He is there if we look. After which the dark is never so dark again.

CHRISTMAS DAY
Christ enters the real world

INTRODUCTION

Some time ago I was reminded[1] of a group of soldiers on active service looking forward to Christmas. They were counting the days. They could scarcely believe that in a matter of hours now they would be sleeping in a bed, eating at a table; there would be privacy, cleanness, kind consideration from everyone in the family circle. Surely the experience would be like heaven on earth. But the homecoming was a failure, or almost a failure. The surrounding comfort seemed unreal, the soft bed out of place, even the kindness so generously given, hurt. That was the unease of the whole situation. They did not feel *in place* till they were back with the terror, the dirt and the drill.

1. *Christmas was not an idyll*
I can't help thinking that Christmas often fails to speak to us because we have made it pretty, soft and tinkling. Not that I

---

[1] By a sermon of Helmut Thielicke's in *Christ and the meaning of Life* (James Clarke), p. 16, which gave me the idea of this sermon.—Author.

see any reason why we should not all step out for a few hours at this time of the year into our childhood. It won't do hard business men any harm to sing a few touching little carols, to pull a few crackers, to wear a funny paper hat, to make the children laugh if they want to. It is all to the good that families should gather together today around Christmas trees. And if there are children into whose sense of wonder they can enter, how salutary this can be.

But this is my question. How deep down will all this succeed? Is there really any connection between this Christmassy world we rig up and the real world? Haven't most of us been straining after something we don't believe in, something idyllic, something unreal, something about which we are inwardly uneasy? Shan't we sense that we have got to the place where we belong, the real world, the adult world when we pack up the tinsel, the holly and the Christmas trees; back to the boardroom, back to the daily trek on packed underground trains, back to loneliness in one room, perhaps with a gas ring for a companion. That is real life.

But, you see, I don't think Christmas was an idyll, or was even intended to be an idyll. The child we remember today was homeless. He was shoved off in a stable. Shortly afterwards his parents became refugees on the open road to Egypt, and behind them, Herod's soldiers, nosing out every newborn child to kill it, in the hope of exterminating this one. And it was always like that. This child, when he grew up, was even a fugitive. They hounded him from place to place till last of all he was shoved out of this world, dying on a gallows, the shape of a cross. This man who loved others, all others, till the end of the road, they had no use for him. They shoved him out. Christ and Cross; manger and gallows. They are both made of wood. They are both the same. There was nothing idyllic about Christmas. It was bare. It was cold. It was very rough.

And someone is thinking, Oh, but you are spoiling it. You are killing the light-heartedness. You are minimizing the fun. I don't think I am. I believe Christmas will say something to us at a deep-down level if we see it for what it was before our sentimentality turned it into an idyll. We shall sense strong comfort here, a secure refuge, something which holds us in the real world of grey daylight, a foundation on top of which we can build a safe light-heartedness.

2. *The true message of Christmas*

And what is the message? That Christ came where we are. He did not shout down instructions about what we should do over some 'Intercom. System.' He came and lived where we worry about what is going to happen next in Africa, here where drug addiction is engulfing thousands of 'teenage' Londoners, where we try to do what is right and honourable, but fall down so often that we are almost ashamed to try again. Christ came here himself. He understands how the real world feels, the harsh world, the grey world. He understands everything. He understands you and me.

It is not a pretty pretty world we live in now. Heaven knows what is happening to some political prisoners in South Africa. And I tremble to think what it is really like in Vietnam. How life seems to people today is to be judged from the work of our artists. They are our eyes; and what modern painting, modern music and modern poetry set before us is distortion, disharmony and dissonance. I am not surprised that a pretty pretty Christmas has nothing to say in the 1960s.

APPLICATION

But suppose we look at the real Christmas, at the child shoved out, at the parents fleeing. We are looking, then, at the beginning of one who knows his way around the ruins of our world, at one who was wounded himself, wounded for us. Only one who knows wounds can heal wounds. This is the Christ who is not switched off when in twenty-four hours from now we turn out the electric candles on our Christmas trees of make-believe. The real Christ, the Christ in the wooden crib, the Christ on the wooden Cross knows our world. The loneliness of that old lady in Queen's Gate Terrace.

The sickening terror of being cut off by some 'takeover bid' which the business man fears. Frustration. Shame. Depression. The Christ of the real Christmas comes where I am. That is the strong consolation of this service. God waiting for me. God looking for me. If that is true there will be no flop when this season is over. Christmas has a message for the real world. This is what the Gospel for Christmas tells us, 'He came unto his own, and his own received him not. But as many as received him, to them gave he power to become the sons of God, even to them that believe on his name.'

EPIPHANY 1

Our justification

> St. Luke 2. 52 (NEB) *'As Jesus grew up he advanced in wisdom and in favour with God and men.'*

INTRODUCTION

Did he, do you think? As Jesus grew up did he advance in wisdom and in favour with God and men? And if he did, what difference does it make? What difference will it make to you in your office tomorrow? or in your flat? What difference could it make to a member of the Stock Exchange? or to a physicist? or to a newspaper man in Fleet Street?

There are two questions here. Did Jesus advance in wisdom and stature as the Gospel for today is at pains to tell us? And if he did, what difference does it make?

1. *Did it happen?*

I have to admit I cannot prove it. There is no photograph of Jesus as a boy, no oil painting, not even a pencil sketch, nothing which would allow me to say, 'Well, see for yourself. Isn't it obvious he was far and away ahead of anyone else of his years, look at those eyes.' The truth is, no such pictorial evidence exists. Nor can I say, 'Read through these sentences. Look what Jesus wrote at the age of twelve. Doesn't the very form of this literary work, let alone its content, cry out how outstanding he was?' The truth is, we have no written work from the hand of Jesus, no music he composed, no painting he executed. We have, in fact, no documentary, no tangible evidence, that comes anywhere near *proof* that 'Jesus advanced in wisdom and in favour with God and men.' There is only St. Luke's account to go on, the Gospel for today.

St. Luke, however, is not lightly to be passed over. He was a careful writer. In writing the Book of the Acts of the Apostles, for example, he did not slip up over the diverse titles given to the various officials in the Roman administration, complicated as they were. Luke was careful, orderly and thorough in his work. We cannot, therefore, lightly pass over the account of Jesus' boyhood he has given us. In itself it is striking, anyway. A summary of Jesus' boyhood up to the age of twelve. Next, a story illustrating what he was like at that age. Thirdly, another summary of his life from adolescence to manhood. 'As Jesus grew up he advanced in wisdom and in favour with God and men.'

I expect you remember the illustration. We all remember the illustrations, for instance, in sermons. Here it is about Jesus going up to the Jerusalem Temple with his parents. And how he stayed behind after they had set out for home. 'And when they returned, seeking him, there he was in the Temple surrounded by the teachers, listening to them and putting questions; and all who heard him were amazed at his intelligence, and the answers he gave.'

Yes, we know the story well, but have we 'taken in' its striking points, some implicit, some explicit?

First, there is scarcely anything said about material environment. It is arresting to us who make such a fuss over our bright new schools, all glass and central heating. In fact, you will notice that a great deal of the present planning in education is not about education but about buildings, environment and incipient class distinction. These externals are what we stress.

St. Luke's account, however, ranks the parents as of first importance.

Secondly, you will notice that the child was brought into touch with the established religion of the day. It was established and it was organized. It was also very far from perfect. But Jesus was not allowed to grow up in isolation from the visible organization of religious awareness.

Thirdly, perfect though he was, Jesus was not free from subjection to the authority of his parents. The path to perfection does not lie through complete freedom. Too much freedom can mean too much imperfection. We take this hardly, but this is the implication of today's Gospel.

Fourthly, Jesus did, however, break away from his parents. The process began when he was twelve years old. The breakaway was painful to Mary. The growing independence of the developing child always does hurt good parents. But there cannot be development of personality without the breakaway.

All this means, of course, that Jesus developed in childhood, adolescence and manhood as we develop. He did not begin with a man's mind in a boy's body. Such would be grotesque. He developed gradually, only in his case he was perfect at each stage of development. Perfect baby, perfect boy, perfect young man. And because he developed throughout in constant response to the will of God, without rebellion, his insight into life was quite astonishing. And this, perhaps, is one of the most challenging points of the whole story.

2. What difference does it make?

And someone is thinking, yes, all very interesting, but what difference does it make to me? How will today's Gospel help me as I set off for my work tomorrow, or settle myself to household chores?

But let me 'put it to you.' Don't you sometimes feel the human race is a heartbreaking failure? So much good, so much that is encouraging, such a long and patient struggle for progress, but always somewhere happiness is crushed again by meanness, sordidness and devilry, sometimes by the few, sometimes by the many. The latest we have been told is that we must expect in the world the rise of more leaders of the Hitler mentality, desperate men thrust up from 'the have-nots.' Humanity seems to be a heartbreaking failure.

But is humanity a failure? Hasn't humanity produced Socrates and Charlemagne and Edward the Confessor and Floresnce Nightingale and Albert Schweitzer, and a host of other? And if there were faults in these, and in any others you could list, wasn't there also Jesus Christ whom St. Luke tells us was perfect at every stage of his development? Doesn't Christ justify the human race? Aren't we, as humans, justified by Jesus, that is, by Jesus' very existence? Couldn't we interpret Paul's doctrine of justification by Christ in this way? Doesn't it mean something then?

Suppose we put the matter like this. Here is a school. I have a school in mind. Badly sited. Inadequate playing-fields. Old-fashioned buildings. The Education Authority want to close it down. It appears as a pathetic exhibition of what a school building should be. But look at the scholarships won from that school, some of them brilliant. Don't those few justify the many disappointing scholars? Can you write the school off? Can you dub it a failure?

Jesus, then, the boy Jesus, the man Jesus, developing in the place and manner we have to develop, but developing in perfection is *our* justification. Oh, I know this is apprehended by faith and not as a result of logical proof. But St. Paul did say, 'We sinners are justified *by faith* in Jesus Christ.'

APPLICATION

Let me finish with something simple. Jesus reached the point of quite astonishing insight into life through co-operation with the will of God for him. We, however, are so often tempted to think that such a life of faith and obedience makes a man 'green.' He needs to have 'gone the pace a bit' if he is to develop into a real man. But is this so? Must the eye specialist have suffered affliction in his own eyes to be a good eye doctor? Is it not better that he has perfect eyes before he looks into yours? Jesus, then, achieved his remarkable stature of unbelievable insight into life and people because he had never compromised the right. Doesn't that give you fresh encouragement about the rightness of right living, and the wisdom of right living? I hope it does, because far too often we churchpeople lose our nerve about the worshipping, believing, obeying way of life. It does not make for 'greenness.' It can make for stature. Quite often it makes for giant proportions of character and skill. Won't you let that thought encourage you as a churchman this morning?

EPIPHANY 2

Gaiety

St. John 2. 11 (NEB) ' *This deed at Cana-in-Galilee is the first of the signs by which Jesus revealed his glory and led his disciples to believe in him.*'

INTRODUCTION

On Christmas Eve when I tried to drive into Queen's Gate Mews to fill up with petrol for the holiday period, my way was blocked by a huge six-wheeler tanker. I must have sat behind it in my car for ten minutes, waiting to drive into that narrow street. But I consoled myself by thinking as I looked at the tanker that there would, anyhow, be enough petrol for me. The man on the pumps wouldn't say they had run out. Then the tanker moved. But to my surprise it didn't pull up at the garage at all: it pulled up at the public house opposite. What, in fact, the huge tanker contained was not petrol but beer, and I saw the driver connect a four-inch pipe to a nozzle, and the pumping process began; gallons of beer were pumped into the cellar for the holiday season.

1. *Our Lord's first miracle was to make wine*

Now it is a strange fact that the first miracle St. John records in his Gospel is Christ's production of wine—not a tiny sip, nor even a glassful or a bottleful, but a hundred and twenty gallons of the stuff, and pretty strong at that, I shouldn't wonder, judging from the comments of one who drank it. It is strange, isn't it? Strange especially for those who reckon wine wicked, which I don't, but strange that of all the miracles with which the author of the fourth Gospel might have chosen to begin his account of the story of Jesus, he selected this one of making wine by the bucketful. A hundred and twenty gallons of it.

And it is possible to pile the strangeness on. Because if it is true, as I think it is, that the miracles were not wrought primarily for the comfort of those on whom they were wrought, nor even to display the power of Jesus, but in order to show his glory, that is to say, in order to reveal the visible presence of God in compassion, wisdom and love, then it is all the more strange to choose the making of bucketfuls of wine for the purpose. Why not begin with healing a leper, or forgiving a man's sins, or feeding the hungry? But no, John begins with the story of Jesus turning the water into wine. 'This deed at Cana-in-Galilee is the first of the signs by which Jesus revealed his glory and led his disciples to believe in him.' That is the Gospel for this second Sunday after the Epiphany.

2. *The first meaning of the Kingdom of God*

How do you account for it? I think it can only be accounted for by a willingness to see that Christ wished us to understand first, that the Kingdom of God is a joyous thing; it is like a wedding, not marriage—no, it is like a wedding. That is, an occasion when everyone is wearing his best clothes, everyone is in light-hearted mood, and a great many people there at the wedding (even if some do shed a tear or two) are deep down inside them supremely happy. They feel that something good and right and proper is taking place—a wedding. And they enjoy it. They talk, they laugh, yes, and you've got to admit it, they drink wine.

May I remind you of the story? There was a wedding at Cana in Galilee, and Jesus and his mother and the disciples were invited. But something went wrong. That something is so set in the story as to make it *the* overwhelming calamity at the wedding—the wine ran out. And Jesus' mother, becoming aware of it, told Jesus. And Jesus did nothing at first, but then he turned six large stone jars of water, each containing two or three firkins, that is, at least one hundred and twenty gallons, into wine, or so it seemed. That water there in those stone jars wasn't for drinking, it was used for washing the feet. This is what Jesus turned into wine, such wine, that the master of the ceremonies was amazed when he noted the quality of the wine that came towards the end of the feast.

Now I can't tell you how the miracle was performed. I shouldn't even quarrel with you if you wanted to question some of the details of the story. But what I must ask you to notice is that Christ likened the Kingdom of God to the merriment of a wedding. Where Christ is, there must be life, light and laughter. And if there isn't, he will make it so. That is how he began at Cana in Galilee. It was the first sign. It was the first indication he gave of his glory, and of what God's presence means.

And some people do not like this. Some even detest it. They are afraid of it. They do not want a religion which brings zest, freedom and laughter. After all, it might start poking fun at stuffy old conventions. It might let in some draughts of fresh air to pious opinions. That is what the Pharisees thought. That is why, you can be sure, they went away from hearing about the wedding feast at Cana in Galilee to plot Jesus' destruction. We can't have religion like this. It might upset the *status quo*.

But Jesus' disciples believed in him. The account says so. 'This deed at Cana-in-Galilee is the first of the signs by which Jesus revealed his glory and led his disciples to believe in him.'

In the Victoria and Albert Museum is a little statue, nineteen inches high, made in terra-cotta. It was purchased in 1858 from Paris, and is reckoned to be one of the great sculptures of the Virgin and Child. But no one knows exactly whose work it is. Many suggestions have been made, but there is no certainty except that it is a product of the Italian Renaissance. And when you see it you will laugh as you are meant to laugh. You will laugh because the Child is laughing. He is not looking at his mother, he is looking at you as you look at him, and his face is bubbling with merriment. And Mary, too, is looking at him, her face broken with a smile of tenderness. It is a striking piece. It is called 'The Virgin and the laughing Child.'

Why have we been so slow to grasp the truth that Christ presented the Kingdom of God (which means God's rule in the hearts of men) as a happy experience? And when it isn't happy and buoyant and smiling, something has gone wrong. Is it the devil who takes away laughter, and is it Christ who gives it? And wherever men are deeply happy, there must be the Kingdom of God.

APPLICATION

I come back to this wine. In a moment, in the service of Holy Communion, you will be offered wine. And with it the words, 'The blood of our Lord Jesus Christ which was shed for thee, preserve thy body and soul unto everlasting life.' As you think of the Cross you may think of it sadly. 'The blood of our Lord Jesus Christ which was shed for thee.' But remember this. What represents the blood in the chalice is not water, nor vinegar, it is wine. And wine, as the psalmist sang, 'maketh glad the heart of man.' Christ shed his blood, not to make us sad, but to make us happy. We have not always given that impression, so maybe we need this Gospel for the second Sunday after Epiphany after all. Christ began his ministry by turning water into a hundred and twenty gallons of wine. Surely we cannot fail to see from this what he meant the characteristics of Christian discipleship to be—an experience almost of gaiety.

EPIPHANY 3

No barriers

St. Matthew 8. 11 *'And I say unto you that many shall come from the east and the west, and sit down with Abraham, and Isaac, and Jacob, in the Kingdom of God.'*

INTRODUCTION

One evening when I looked in at 'Panorama' on BBC1, the camera spent a good deal of time showing us 'close-ups' of the faces of people in India and Africa, and we heard their voices. I have to confess they seemed a long way off to me. I don't mean in distance on the earth's surface, but a long way off in manner of life; so much so that I marvelled again at the faith of those pioneers who first took the Christian Gospel to those far off peoples. I wonder how many of us would have said, 'Oh, but look at them, you can't do anything with them!'

1. No racial barrier

The Gospel for today brings to our attention a 'far off' man. That is to say, he was 'far off' from the first followers of Jesus. He was a Roman, an army man, the army, in fact, that was keeping the Jews down. There was no love lost between the Jews and the occupying power. You wouldn't expect it. Moreover, there was a whole world of difference between the Romans and the Jews. Yet none of these differences pinpointed by race proved to be a barrier. Jesus healed this Roman officer's boy.

There are two points to notice about this Roman. First, it was he who made the approach to Jesus across the barrier. It wasn't the other way round. Similarly, it was the Wise Men who travelled to see the Infant Christ, not the other way round. So the Syrophoenician woman came seeking on behalf of her daughter. And the Greeks approached Philip, 'Sir, we would see Jesus.' First, the citadel of the Christian way was broken into *from the outside* by outsiders. The time came when the whole Church, and when St. Peter himself, took the Gospel to outsiders, but he needed a special revelation from heaven to make him take this unprecedented step (as recorded in Acts 10). This Roman, however, saw the truth long before. The remarkable fact is that sometimes an outsider can see more clearly the purpose of God in the world than those enclosed in a narrow form of ecclesiasticism. Jesus found it remarkable. He remarked, 'I have not found so great faith, no, not in Israel... many shall come from the east and west and sit down in the Kingdom of God.'

Secondly, we should note how the Roman army officer saw into the nature of Jesus' ministry by examining his own. He said to himself, 'I have authority. I can say to this man, "Do this," and to that man, "Do that." My belief is this Jesus can do the same. No, there is no need for Jesus to come in person to my house to heal my fever-tossed boy. He can simply say the word, and the boy will be healed.' That is to say, because of his overwhelming authority Christ can heal from the outside, he can heal afar off, he can heal far off peoples. And that is the message of the Epiphany. The Christian Gospel is for all peoples. There are no racial barriers. And so the Church, wherever it has been true to its Lord, has been a missionary-hearted church.

Our *first* lesson today, therefore, is to sweep from our minds any thoughts of racial barriers to the scope of the Christian Gospel. They should not exist.

2. *No social barrier*

Our *second* lesson is to recognize another barrier that might exist, and to sweep this away also. The one I have in mind is not easy to define. It could be called the barrier of class, or of the Establishment, or of the manual/non-manual worker divide.

Sometimes we are tempted to think that our social barriers are impenetrable. Perhaps there is no place where this judgement might seem more justified than in Haarlem in New York City. The police almost despair of keeping that place in control, let alone creating anything positive out of the human material, riddled as it is by drug-taking, and every known form of perversion and violence. But in the last few years, as the result of the work of some young men, a worshipping community has been formed in Haarlem. Bruce Kenrick's book, *Come out the wilderness*, tells the remarkable story. It is worth reading. No, not even this tough social barrier is impenetrable. The Gospel transcends it.

3. No denominational barrier

Thirdly, Christian denominations can be a barrier, a barrier, that is, to the free flowing of the Spirit of Christ in a community.

Thank God, in the last twenty years, in the last five years, many of these barriers are coming down. The movement towards Church Unity is running on. May it run on yet more and more.

APPLICATION

What is the message for the third Sunday after Epiphany? Let none of us label anyone an outsider from Christ, because of race, class or denomination. Christ is for all. All are for Christ. And let us see that our Church represents this catholic, this universal, this evangelical, this missionary approach in all that we do, for it is clearly after the mind of him we profess to serve, our Lord and Saviour, Jesus Christ.

EPIPHANY 4

Christ's strange authority

> St. Matthew 8. 34 *'And behold, all the city came out to meet Jesus: and when they saw him, they besought him that he would depart from their borders.'*

INTRODUCTION

During the last few years we have become accustomed to hearing of leaders of one kind or another being asked to leave a country; it might be South Africa, Ghana or Czechoslovakia. It comes as a surprise, however, to hear that Jesus was once asked to leave a country, as a kind of undesirable citizen. But he was. Indeed, it is the story in the Gospel for today, Epiphany 4, 'And behold, all the city came out to meet Jesus: and when they saw him, they besought him that he would depart from their borders.'

First, I propose that we look at the kind of leader Jesus was. Secondly, that we observe why he was asked to leave. And thirdly, what these two points together tell us about the nature of Jesus' authority.

1. *The kind of leader Jesus was*

This is depicted for us by St. Matthew in three stories strung together. The story of Jesus stilling the storm, the story of his cure of the demoniacs in Gadara, and the story of his forgiveness of a man's sins, and the cure of his paralysis. The first two of these stories form the Gospel for today.

(*a*) First we notice that Jesus was a leader who could *rebuke*. All three stories show him rebuking. He rebuked the wind and the sea, and 'there was a great calm.' He rebuked the demons of madness from the two possessed, and ejected them. He also overrode the question of the scribes who dared to criticize his authority to forgive sins. Jesus was a leader who exercised his authority and was prepared to rebuke those who resisted it. We need to notice this. There cannot be leadership without rebuke. Writing to young Timothy, the new leader Paul wrote: 'Reprove, rebuke, exhort with all longsuffering and teaching.' A leader who agrees with everybody in everything is no leader.

(*b*) Secondly, he was a leader who stood head and shoulders above his fellows in both *skill and stature*. In these three stories the disciples were swamped with panic in the storm-tossed ship, but Jesus was calmly sleeping. The community in Gadara fled in terror from the two maniacs in the graveyard, but Jesus went forward and confronted them personally. Back at Capernaum the scribes were haggling over who could forgive sins, but Jesus cut through the whole theological tangle by practising forgiveness, and demonstrating its effectiveness by causing a paralytic to get up and walk. A leader is no leader unless he can do things other men cannot do. Leadership rests in accomplishment, and not in status.

(c) Thirdly, a leader who really leads must care for his followers. This, Jesus did. He stilled the storm on the lake to give his terror-struck disciples peace. He exorcized those demoniacal men in the graveyard in Gadara, in order to ease the life both of them and the whole community they were terrorizing. He forgave the paralytic's sins and, in so doing, healed his legs, because he wished to grant the man a future life. Jesus cared for people. Napoleon and Wellington were leaders because of what they could do. But Nelson was greater; he not only towered above his fellows in daring accomplishments, but really cared for his men. In mid-Mediterranean, hard on the heels of the French, he would stop to pick up a man washed overboard. The navy never forgot that.

2. *Why was he asked to leave?*

Jesus, then, was an outstanding leader, measured by any yardstick, but over in Gadara, and in the eastern side of the lake of Galilee, *they asked him to leave the country*. 'And behold, all the city came out to meet Jesus: and when they saw him, they besought him that he would depart from their borders.' Why was this? That is what we must now examine.

And the question isn't difficult. Indeed, the way Matthew sets down the story, in comparison with Mark, makes the point obvious. St. Mark gives us quite a 'close-up' of the cured man. St. Matthew only lets us know of the cure by inference. What he settles on is the fact that the cure of the demoniacs caused a herd of swine to panic, and rush down the steep into the sea, and to perish in the waters. That is why the whole community came out to meet Jesus. A couple of maniacs might be restored to sanity, but when those swine rushed into the sea, a whole lot of money went down the drain.

So they asked Jesus to depart. Jesus was alright, but not if he caused money to go down the drain. It is good to read about men like Jesus, but let him not come too close. From Gadara's point of view Jesus was splendid, on the other side of the lake! But he is too costly to have too close. All the city, therefore, 'came out to meet Jesus: and when they saw him, they besought him to depart from their borders.'

3. *What do these two points together tell us about the nature of Jesus' authority?*

Remember, we see him going. Without resistance, the rebuking, talented, caring Christ departs. If you have imagination, you can see him now, sitting in the stern of the ship, sailing back to Capernaum, the disciples only too keen to quit Gadara. Perhaps his hand was trailing in the water.

What does this mean? It means Jesus never forces his presence on anyone. That is the difference between the authority of Christ and the authority of a dictator. Far too often benefactors have forced benefits on recipients which they do not want, after which the benefactors are viewed as tyrants, and the good spirit departs. Christ never forces. If we do not want him to stay, he will certainly depart. It calls for a view of omnipotence different from the ordinary.

> Rabbi, begone! thy powers
> Bring loss to us and ours.
> Our ways are not as thine.
> Thou lovest men, we—swine.
> Oh, get you hence, Omnipotence,
> And take this fool of thine!
> His soul? What care we for his soul?
> What good to us that thou hast made him whole
> Since we have lost our swine?
>   JOHN OXENHAM

APPLICATION

What is the lesson of Epiphany 4? God will come into the life of any man. There are no barriers, no outsiders to Christ. He will visit on the other side of the lake, the other side of the divide between the respectable and the outcasts. No iron curtain is final for the Spirit of God. Only one situation will prevent the divine presence, the resistance of the human heart.

Let us understand the nature of God's life-giving authority. It can be resisted. May we not resist it. Then we experience the benefits he undoubtedly brings to the community, and to individuals as well.

EPIPHANY 5

Masterly inactivity

St. Matthew 13. 30 *'Let both grow together until the harvest.'*

INTRODUCTION

This is bad news for hotheads, men of zeal, men of action, 'do-gooders,' all religious enthusiasts and reformers. It seems to say hands off God's Kingdom. Why?

1. *Because the Church is not experienced as a pure society*
There is a story of a young man visiting Charles Spurgeon, the great eighteenth-century Baptist preacher, and asking him where he could find the pure church. Spurgeon replied to the effect that there were good, honest and sincere worshippers in the Metropolitan Tabernacle, but also some unworthy, insincere and sinful members. No, Spurgeon did not think his was the pure church. Furthermore, he said, if by any chance you do discover the pure church, and it is unlikely, be careful not to join it, because the moment you do, it will immediately become tainted.

This is the truth. The Church is composed of sinners. Redeemed sinners, no doubt, but sinners all the same. Nothing in the world is perfect. Not even the Church, not even the manifestation or embodiment of the Kingdom of God. And this accords with our experience of life. It should warn us off expecting the impossible. It should temper all zeal for reformation, even when reformation should be carried out.

2. *Because we do not know who the heretics are*
In this parable of the Wheat and the Tares, the servants were very anxious to rush into the fields and rip up the weeds. But in the early stages of growth it is not easy to differentiate between wheat and darnel. There are churchmen now ready to excommunicate all the Demythologizers, Existentialists and New Theologians, but are we sure they are all heretics? The advice of the parable is, time will tell. 'Let both grow together till the harvest.'

3. *Because it is very easy to uproot tender Christians*
It is easy, of course, to offend tender Christians by leaving anomalies in the Church. Young people, especially, being idealistic, see hypocrisy round every corner. But we are more likely to uproot tender Christians by exhibitions of ruthlessness. The Kingdom of Christ is a kingdom of love. Harsh action can never be right, even in the presence of goodness.

CONCLUSION

The lesson, then, is to trust God concerning his Kingdom. We cannot improve upon his method of operation in the world. After all, he let the enemy come and sow the tares. Christians must be patient. They must wait God's time. There is such a thing as masterly inactivity; but it requires faith in God.

EPIPHANY 6

Deceivers

St. Matthew 24. 24 *'There shall arise false Christs.'*

INTRODUCTION

In recent years housewives have been warned against those plausible agents for household gadgets, who ensnare the unwary into signing agreements to purchase, the terms of which are suppressed. These men are deceivers. Going from door to door they deceive innocent women, involving them in predicaments of which they never thought.

The Gospel for today warns us against deceivers of another sort. They try to sell us Christianity which is not the genuine article. And so we need to be put on our guard.

1. *Beware of religious talk which seems to appeal greatly to signs and wonders*

There *are* gifts of healing in the Church, but if some new organization clamours for allegiance, and to substantiate its claims relies heavily on accounts of bodily healings, trances, second sight and psychological power, distrust it. It is a deceiver. The signs of the presence of Christ are not signs and wonders, but Christian character.

2. *Beware of involved explanations*

A typical argument runs, 'I know it does not appear on the surface as if this is Christian, but if you look carefully into the matter, you will find it is so.' Today's Gospel puts the matter like this. 'Wherefore, if they shall say unto you, "Behold, he is in the desert; go not forth: Behold, he is in the secret chambers; believe it not."' Why? Because when Christ is present in a life, a movement or an organization, no complicated explanation will be required. When the lightning shines, there is no need for careful reasoning to show that it really is lightning. Everybody sees it. Everybody recognizes it. So is the presence of Christ. We must not be deceived, therefore, by rationalization. At present, this has pointed reference to certain loose behaviour, which some try to justify by specious arguments. Do not be deceived.

CONCLUSION

If we are truly Christian, if the Church is true to its Lord, no complicated commendations will be necessary. Whom we serve will be obvious. If not, it could be that even we are deceiving ourselves.

SEPTUAGESIMA

Life and logic

St. Matthew 20. 9 (NEB) *'Those who had started work an hour before sunset came forward, and were paid the full day's wage.'*

INTRODUCTION

I wouldn't like to see the rumpus there would be if the passage of scripture appointed for today's Gospel were put into practice just as it is. It is all about some labourers brought into a vineyard an hour before sunset, that is, an hour before it was time to 'knock off,' and they received precisely the same wages as the men who had been 'at it' since sunrise. I wonder what the unions would say. I know what the labourers would *do*. They would all queue up for work next day at 5.0 p.m. Why not? This lunatic employer gives you the same pay whenever you turn up.

The whole story is so fantastic, so illogical, it forces you to search for a meaning. The speaker wasn't crazy. What, then, could he mean by presenting a crazy story?

1. *Logic is not the final arbiter in life*

One thing he meant is that logic is not the final arbiter in life. We sometimes think it is, especially we men.

Let me illustrate this. Here are two people meeting in the street. They haven't seen each other for six months. When they meet, why do they grab each other's hand for a moment and shake it up and down? Let us be logical. It won't help the blood circulation! But a great deal in life is illogical.

Here is a man who has married a frail girl. Far more logical that he should have visited the local doctor to procure the woman with the best medical history, or the best vital statistics, and marry her.

The truth is, logic is reduced to a very minor role in some of the biggest issues in life. We get born, the whole race goes on as a result of actions in which logic plays only the smallest part.

I am not going on from here to poke fun at the scientists. Results can only be obtained on the laboratory bench by the application of logic. And a doctor would be useless in diagnosis if he couldn't think back logically from your symptoms to the cause of your illness, and then on to the cure.

But this is where we go wrong, when we think that logic must play a major role *everywhere*. It isn't true. One of the places where it isn't true is in the great spheres of birth, death, life, love, hate, fear, depression, joy; and what a huge sphere it is.

Jesus, then, told this fantastically illogical parable so that we shall reduce logic to its proportions in the understanding of life.

2. *Eleventh-hour conversions*

Jesus also told this parable so that we shall change our minds about people who turn to religion when they are dying, or at least when life narrows in, or the bottom falls out of happiness, or some national calamity looms up on the horizon. We feel pretty cool about this sort of thing. Cool, perhaps, about the penitent thief, penitent because he was dying. We like the stiff upper lip, the head bloody but unbowed, no whining when things go against a man. We like him to take it like a man.

But does the unbending attitude in life get a man very far? May it not make him wooden, insensitive, even stupid, a man without insight, a man without vision. Stiffness doesn't make for happiness.

On the basis of logic God ought, of course, to open his arms only to those who have never grown slack about Holy Communion, but in the laboratory of life, logic doesn't take us very far; and because God wants to go far, and be a living God, he doesn't measure with logic, he measures with love. He will receive that old fiddler in the flat upstairs whenever he turns to seek his presence, just as he will receive you and receive me.

3. *Creation and Redemption are gifts*

By the time Jesus has cleared away from my mind all the overdone reliance on logic by his fantastically illogical parable of the Labourers of the Vineyard, I feel I haven't much left to chalk up in my favour, which apparently he will notice. The late-comers will be taken in just as I shall, who have been a regular churchgoer since I was a choir-boy at the age of seven.

So I come at last, and it takes some doing, to learn that the Christian religion has its roots, not in my merits, but in Christ's love, work and activity. That puts me in the proper place where I should be, the proper frame of mind, the proper frame of heart. From that place I am willing to receive the salvation which God gives me. God's creation is a gift. All the loveliness of God's world we think of at Septuagesima is a gift. Likewise, salvation is a gift. God's gift. And when we see it like that, forced to see it by the illogical parable of the Labourers of the Vineyard, we become Christians without a proud look and a high stomach, the only kind that is really Christian.

SEXAGESIMA

How to listen

St. Luke 8. 18 (NEB) *'Take care, then, how you listen.'*

INTRODUCTION

At first this seems strange, 'Take care, then, how you listen.' It might seem impossible. You either listen or you don't listen. But is this so? A girl waiting every post for a letter from her boy-friend does not hear the postman's steps as they draw nearer down the street in the same way as her father, reading the newspaper. She hears with expectancy. He just hears. So there are different ways of listening.

And this is true of our listening to the word of God, however that word comes; whether in an event that takes place, the advice of a friend, or through the Epistle, Gospel, or the sermon in church. We may not listen so as to produce results from our listening.

Now the Gospel for Sexagesima Sunday, the 'Parable of the Sower,' or the 'Parable of the Soils' tells us how to listen.

1. *We must listen so that something 'goes in.'*
All of us have had the experience of talking, when suddenly we realize that our friend isn't listening. He hears, but nothing is 'going in.' The word of God will not 'go into' the lives of people if they are always 'on the go.' Endless rushing about makes our lives like a pathway trodden hard with hurrying feet. No seed can possibly find a lodging where it can grow. To listen to the word of God we must make times of keeping still.

2. *We must weigh carefully what is heard*
It would be possible to be thrilled by the language of a sermon, and go back time and time again for more, and not hear the word of God. The same can be said even of Bible-reading, for the scriptures consist of noble prose. Hearing of that kind, however, would be like a plant that suddenly springs up in the warm sunshine, but because it has no depth of soil in which rooting is possible, it quickly withers in the mid-day sun. When we listen to the word of God we must reach down with our minds through the form and the content, down to the deep roots which have their origin at a gibbet outside a city wall, and a Man there praying, 'Father, forgive them, for they know not what they do.' Any enthusiasm apart from this is misplaced.

3. *We need to listen so as to give what we hear space in our minds*
Little value is to be found in rushing into church at the last minute from cleaning the car, or rushing out after the service to finish it. Our minds in such cases are like plants surrounded by weeds. The word of God has been heard, but a plant can only grow if it is surrounded by space. We must clear the ground around the word of God. We must listen in prepared spaces of silence.

APPLICATION

'Take care, then, how you listen.' Take care that the week is not crammed with *endless* activity. That way comes spiritual death. Take care that high-sounding religious phrases are not confused with the Christian gospel. The Gospel tells of receiving through giving, life through death, victory through sacrifice, strong teaching!

Take care not to cram some devotional exercise into some already crammed programme. The word of God must have space.

QUINQUAGESIMA

A broken thing

> St. Luke 18. 42 *'Receive thy sight: thy faith hath saved thee.'*

INTRODUCTION

When I was a small boy, I longed for a certain present for my birthday, but when it came, and I opened the parcel, the present was broken. I found the occasion hard to bear. Now suppose, I say suppose, someone had deliberately sent me a broken present, I should have found it impossible to understand, let alone bear.

1. *Our problem*

This is our problem. Whenever we enter a church the first sight that greets our eyes is a man broken on a cross. Not a warrior king leading us as a triumphant army to possess the heavenly city, but a man whose life is poured out in pain.

And when we come to the Church's chief service of worship, we are offered a piece of broken bread. And if what we are given is a perfectly-shaped wafer, one of those wafers has been broken before the distribution takes place. The reason is because on the night before Jesus was broken on the cross, he broke bread, and gave it to his disciples, saying, 'Do this in remembrance of me.'

Perhaps we find this central presence of a broken man difficult to receive. We are not the only ones. The twelve disciples found this difficult. The Gospel for today tells us that when Jesus told them of his coming death, they simply could not understand.

2. *Our answer*

This incident is then followed by the story of a blind man begging Jesus for his sight. Why is the story so placed? Who is the blind man? It is the disciples. Perhaps it is us. We cannot understand the reason for the brokenness.

But the man's blindness was overcome. Not by rationalization. Not by logic. He was enabled to see by asking for sight, and by trusting Christ for sight. Then he heard the words of liberation, 'Receive thy sight: thy faith hath saved thee.'

How do we begin to perceive the meaning of the brokenness? Not by a process of reasoning, but by self-committal. The existentialists are more right than the logicians. We come to know by committing ourselves.

APPLICATION

One way of expressing this all-important self-committal is by receiving the broken bread now. And, remember, resurrection takes place, according to the Gospel, at the place of brokenness.

LENT 1

The use of power

INTRODUCTION

I know it isn't easy here in the busy streets of London. I know it isn't easy in the ornate beauty of this church, but I would like you at least to try and visualize for a moment a bare mountain top. You know how it is, first the wooded foothills, then grass, then for the last few hundred feet, rock, scree and broken stones. There is nothing soothing on a mountain top, no shade from the sun, no shelter from the wind. But what is most obvious to any human being who climbs up there, is the silence, such silence that you can almost feel it. Nothing moves, except perhaps a stone you have dislodged, or the occasional swish of the wings of a bird passing at that height.

But the Gospel for today urges us to look more closely. There is a man up there. We have to look closely because he doesn't move. His body is still, absolutely still. Clearly, he is not concerned with climbing the rock face, neither is he intent upon those cardboard-like villages in the valley below: his attention is fixed upon something on the screen of his own mind. A shut door of a carpenter's shop, never to be opened by him again. A woman's wistful face, his mother's, watching him wending his way from home life in Nazareth for ever. A hot crowd by the Jordan river, a zealous preacher, the waters of the Jordan river let trickle over the faces of the penitents, the same water let trickle over his own face. And then the overwhelming consciousness of strength in his person, spiritual strength, moral strength, strength that he could use.

But why is he up there, alone with the sky, the scree and the silence? The answer is, because that is the only way to stay strong. A man who runs away from himself to the crowd is useless to the crowd. Only he who is at home with himself in the silence is sufficiently strong not to be trampled on by the pressing of the public. And the startling lesson is—Jesus needed that toughening of silence. How much more then, you! how much more me! If we are to give any attention at all to the spiritual development of our persons, and this, I take it, is the meaning of Lent, we shall have to make arrangements to be absolutely alone.

1. *Bread*

What did Jesus see up there on the canvas of his mind, in the silence of the mountain? He saw that he had power to feed people. He could feed those children down in the village, too weak through malnutrition even to play. He could feed those women whose eyes had grown dead from the endless search for food that wasn't there. He could feed those men grown callous by the emptiness of their stomachs.

But he decided on that mountain that he would not *give* bread, he would only share bread. He would sit at any man's table, and any man could sit at his, but he would not sweep by as in a carriage casting out largesse. Largesse degrades. Jesus intended to uplift. So he never gives with patronage. The greatest you can do for a man is to help him help himself. There would be no charity with patronage in the ministry of Jesus. He determined it on the mountain.

2. *Excitement*

Man, however, does not only live by bread. He needs excitement. Football pools give drab workers excitement. Jesus could give excitement. He could throw himself from the topmost pinnacle of the temple. He could come down from the cross. There is life through excitement, but not eternal life. Excitement can even be ultimately degrading. So Jesus determined not to give excitement in his ministry. He determined to be sparing of miracle. Nor does God grant all our prayers. Otherwise we should ask for the whole world, and gain the whole world—and lose our own soul! Christ will not rule by excitement.

3. *Government*

Power to feed. Power to excite. Jesus knew he also had power to govern. Some governors exercise their rule by removing all power to rebel in their subjects, sometimes almost all power to speak or criticize. Not so Christ. A man can spit in the face of Christ on the cross, and walk away unharmed. God will not smite him for rebellion. God lets us deny his existence because he will not keep us little men below the jackboot of his authority. He did not come to make us little men. He determined that upon the mountain.

APPLICATION

You have power. I have power. There is power of position, power of personality (male and female), power of intellect.

How will you use it? You men, head over an office. You women, head of a household. Will you use your position to crush people's individuality? Will you patronize? Will you tamper with personality? How will you use your power? Jesus needed silence on the mountain top to make decisions for himself. Do you think you do not need such times of solitude? Do you not need what Lent provides?

LENT 2

Love through rules

INTRODUCTION

May I ask you to visualize a young man aged about nineteen. He is quite normal, has a good home background, and is now at the university. He has never been quite so free as he is now, but freedom, he discovers, is not as light as he imagined it to be. It, in fact, carries some heavy problems. For instance, there is that girl who comes to see him from time to time in his rooms. He likes her. It cannot be said that he is in love with her, but he would be sorry if she didn't come. She *is* a girl. Little by little it dawns on him that she need not go home at night. There are rules, of course, in his college. But there are also back stairs and windows, giving on to the street. Even a girl could manage that. What is he to do? Problems like this are two a penny in the 1960's. But why is it a problem? Because nowadays it is reckoned that problem situations cannot be solved by rules of moral behaviour. Everyone has to decide for himself in the situation in which he finds himself. And some Christian leaders follow the same line. They say there is only one law, the law of love, and each individual has to see how it applies to the particular situation in which he finds himself. So this nineteen-year-old is under an obligation to act with Christian love towards this girl, and to decide whether or not keeping her for the night is consistent with that.

1. *Now what attitude did Jesus take to rules?*
Did he recognize that they have a place in guiding us over matters of conduct? We turn now to look at the Gospel for today. It is about a Syrophoenician woman, that is, a Gentile woman, seeking Jesus on behalf of her daughter who was a lunatic. What problems that presented to the woman and her household! But Jesus would do nothing to meet her need. We cannot assert that she did not press her claim. There was no misunderstanding what she wanted. The disciples even grew weary of her persistence. 'Send her away,' they said to Jesus, 'for she crieth after us.' But he would not relent even at their request. 'I was not sent, but unto the lost sheep of the house of Israel.' Such was his reply. Still the woman persisted with a direct appeal. The account says, 'She worshipped him, saying, "Lord, help me."' We can see in imagination her upturned face, perhaps with tears running down her cheeks. But Jesus said, 'It is not right to take the children's bread, and to cast it to dogs.' And no amount of explaining can explain away the strength of that refusal. The woman was an outsider, a Gentile, a dog to the chosen people. Jesus made it clear he was refusing because of what she was—an outsider.

And we are amazed. Perhaps even a little shocked. Did not Christ love all men! Did not his love reach out and beyond even the last limit? Are we not always saying this? Did he not die for all upon the Cross? Did he trouble to inquire if that penitent thief up on the cross beside him had true Jewish blood, when he promised, 'Today, thou shalt be with me in paradise'? Was there ever any love like our Lord's since the world began? Why then this refusal of this poor heathen mother on behalf of her daughter? The answer is, he had made a rule for his ministry, and he had made that rule in the light of the conventions of his day, and he would not lightly break either. What was his rule? It was to restrict his ministry during his lifetime to the Jewish people. Not that it was always to be so restricted. It was destined to reach in his purpose to the ends of the world, but during his lifetime he was to work only in that narrow sphere of one nation in two provinces, Galilee and Judaea. Why? Because only if his gospel was firmly rooted *somewhere* could it ever finally flourish *everywhere*. The day would come when the national boundaries of his message would be burst for ever, but that day would not dawn if he burst *too soon* the curtain Jews recognized between themselves and every Gentile people.

Yet, in the end, Jesus did heal the woman's daughter. He healed her because of her persistence, and because of her faith. He healed on exactly the same ground as any woman of the purest Jewish blood. It is faith that draws down the grace of Christ, not pedigree, sanctity or status.

2. *What are the lessons?*
(a) *The conventions of society are not to be blindly set aside*
It was wrong for the Jews to have no dealings with the Gentiles, but to fly in the face of conventions does not always bring good. We must work gradually and patiently. We must not be too far ahead of public opinion. We must respect what people think, even if we disagree. And conventions and customs are not all stupid. Throughout the ages, certain ways have been found to be the best ways in experience of dealing with certain situations. They are, in fact, accumulated wisdom crystallized out in the form of customs. They may need changing because times have changed, but there was reason behind them. We have to remember this when we come to consider ecclesiastical questions like Intercommunion, and political questions like self-government of former dependencies. To 'jump the gun' is not wise.

(b) *Love can be expressed through rules*
Let us face the point with an example. Here is a beggar who comes to my door. He is dirty, unshaven and lazy. How can I love him emotionally? All my sentiments react in the complete opposite direction. But my Christian love dictates that I should do to him as I would like him to do to me, if the situation were reversed, and I were the beggar. I have, then, a duty to my neighbour. To do this duty *is* to love him. And what that duty is, is summed up in six commandments or

rules, including, 'Thou shalt not steal,' 'Thou shalt not commit adultery,' 'Thou shalt not bear false witness.' I as a Christian express my love to the community by making and observing rules, whereby people are not exploited. Jesus made rules for his ministry, because he wished his love to reach to all men. Rules are most often the way, the only way, by which love can be expressed.

3. *Rules have not, however, the final word*

Jesus was loath to break the rule of his ministry, not to minister to Gentiles, but he *did* break it to meet a case of individual need. He healed the Syrophoenician's daughter. In the end, people must be given priority over systems, be they ecclesiastical or political.

APPLICATION

Rules, especially the ten commandments, can never be lightly set aside. That young man in the college will be wise, every one of us will be wise, to seek out first in every situation, how we can obey them, because they are the means of expressing love to our neighbours. But rules are never an end in themselves. They may have to be broken to meet a human need, but we must be careful the breaking *does* meet a need, and is not simply pandering to our own weaknesses.

LENT 3

The peril of emptiness

> St. Luke 11. 24-26 (NEB) *'When an unclean spirit comes out of a man it wanders over the deserts seeking a resting-place; and finding none, it says, "I will go back to the home I left." So it returns and finds the house swept clean, and tidy. Off it goes and collects seven other spirits more wicked than itself, and they all come in and settle down; and in the end the man's plight is worse than before.'*

I can picture it, can't you? The builder's lorry drawn up by the front door of the house. You never saw such a mess as was discovered when the prospective buyers looked in. Pigeons, rats, moths, beetles, even a couple of owls at the top of the staircase. And damp, of course, had risen. In places it was even unsafe to tread on the floorboards. Walls peeling, windows broken. But the builders put it all right. It took months, and the bill was a big one, but the old house looked smart again, clean, decorated and in good repair. As it happened, however, the prospective occupiers couldn't take possession. The wife fell ill, and they were ordered abroad. Did the house remain clean and in good repair? You know it didn't. If the buyers were unable to occupy it they should have let it. Only an occupied house has a chance of being maintained. An unoccupied one will simply be a refuge for all the pests, vermin and fungus nature can provide. It will be as bad, if not worse than it was before.

Outside the Church of England today there stands a builder's lorry. You never saw such an army of repairers skip from its inside, as when it stopped before the entrance. They find a truly astonishing mixture of things they reckon wrong. Old-fashioned hymns, outworn organizations, fetters binding it to the state, feudal forms of government, a liturgy in Elizabethan English, creeds embodying thought-patterns one thousand five hundred years old, even pernicious ideas among the rank and file, like believing in a God 'up there,' or a God 'out there.' How they leap to the spring-cleaning, and repairing and the plastering.

And there is, of course, need for reform. Last week I saw a whole area being rebuilt with ultra-modern housing, and in the midst stood a nineteenth-century church. You never saw such a decayed museum piece. It was a pile of red bricks on an island of asphalt, surrounded by twelve-foot railings with knobs on. How could you even expect residents from those new glass and chromium houses even to look at that monstrosity, let alone enter it?

And I only mention buildings. There is much else besides bricks and mortar that could do with replacement in the established Church. But this is my problem. When the reformers have worn themselves out with reforming zeal in the Church of England, and it looks clean, modern and tidy, what will they put inside, what worship, what prayer, what preaching? Will they give attention to this?

What I long to see is the Church going on to lay hold of a spiritual interpretation of life, and showing it is necessary. We live in an age dominated by the material, but that dominance is proving itself to be no saviour. Last Thursday there appeared in the newspaper a leader on why the £ is weak. I prophesied when I read it the flood of correspondence that would follow, and I was right. This *is* the sore spot. In a materialistically-minded age it is in the material field that failure makes itself felt. Put our whole trust in things, and before long, things become less available. We shall never get our national life healthy unless we pay more heed than we have done to principles like honesty, self-sacrifice, diligence and thought for other people, and I see no possibility at all of those spiritual virtues being incorporated in the life of our people without a Christ to inspire them, focus them and nourish them.

But what do some of our reformers offer us? What do they put inside our cleaned up, reformed, freshly-garnished churches? Some of them put a social Gospel, that is to say, a religious brand of public welfare. Something which fits the Town Hall, and is right and proper in the Town Hall, and is to be encouraged and supported in the Town Hall, but is no proper tenant of the House of God. It simply leaves it empty, swept and tidy.

Others offer a 'religionless Christianity,' something so vague, so abstract, so demythologized, it is difficult for ordinary people even to see what it is, let alone lay hold of it. This, too, leaves the Church empty, a prey to whatever strange tenants may choose to come to dwell there.

Churches are only doing their jobs if they not only make us see, but come to admire, a man who stood on a mountain top and determined how he would go through with his life. And the crowds fawned on him, turned their backs on him, accepted healing from his hands, and lifted no finger when those hands were nailed up to a cross. Yet there was no whimper from his lips, no weakening, no refusal to help even those who had no religion in their training. Always, for ever and beyond, he was the man for others; and when they took his battered corpse down from the cross, and laid it in a tomb, on Easter Day they found that tomb empty. Death did not defeat this man. I believe churches will be more full of useless clutter than they were before the bandwagon of reforming zealots drew up at our door, *unless* somehow, somewhere, by some means we can be made to see again the proper man, the man Christ Jesus in our world.

Perhaps there is a word here in the story of the empty house, for us as individuals. It would be possible for us to use Lent as a mere season for life emptying. No theatres, no smoking, no alcohol, no parties, and imagine that we were doing well. But nature abhors a vacuum. If there is not some positive laying hold of spiritual principles, some greater awareness of the reality of the other world, some clearer vision and admiration of the Christ himself, what profit will Lent bring? Different habits will simply replace those temporarily banished, and we may find ourselves in worse bondage than before.

For community, for Church, and for individual alike, only one course will save us, and that is a way of life lived in the steps of Jesus our master. That is what I understand by Christianity. That, I think, is what ordinary people of England understand by Christianity. And unless our churches, our priests, and our people give some more recognizable blasts on *this* trumpet, our ecclesiastical organization for all the reformation will dismally fail. What we need is a fresh hold on Christ again, the Christ who makes the spiritual world real, and the issue of life hopeful and glorious.

LENT 4

God recognizes ordinary things

St. John 6. 5 (NEB) *'Where are we to buy bread to feed these people?'*

INTRODUCTION

That is surprising. I mean it is surprising according to our common estimate of spiritually-minded people that Jesus should have asked, 'Where are we to buy bread to feed these people?' You would think he would be concerned perpetually with ideas like the Kingdom of God, or the Resurrection, or what we call the absolute values. The verse, however, tells us something important about God.

1. *God recognizes our basic fleshly needs*
How much, how little, would Beethoven's Piano Concerto No. 4 uplift, if the concert hall was stone cold, or we had no supper? When the 5,000 appeared before Jesus, he did not enlarge on the wonders of the spiritual life, he fed them. He spent much time on people with ordinary ills, troubles and fears, even on a domestic crisis at a wedding party. Real Christianity that follows in the steps of Christ is always very human. Jesus taught us to pray, 'Give us this day our daily bread.'

2. *God recognizes that it is often the small worries that defeat us*
When the 5,000 gathered on the northern end of Lake Tiberias, Jesus knew that what was really at the back of their minds was the lateness of the hour, how would they journey home, would their wives and children make the journey. So he met them at the point of the small nagging worries at the backs of their minds. We can often face the big issues of life as big people in a big way. It is the little things that 'get us down.' God knows this. We can, therefore, approach God in prayer about the little things, they are not too little for God. He knows how *they* can make us fall.

3. *God takes the ordinary things to produce extraordinary results*

There was nothing very grand about five barley loaves and two small fishes, let alone after a boy had carried them about for a whole hot day. But that is what the Christ of God took to feed a hungry crowd.

APPLICATION

Every one of us who is a real Christian should expect miracles to happen in ordinary affairs. This is where we want miracles, because, being human, we get 'bogged down' in the ordinary. Of course, we can always explain away miracles if we want to. This is the point. What do we want? Most of us want to believe in God. Life is so flat without God. And what the Gospel for today teaches, is that God is not too lofty to be concerned with lowly things. The divine does not cancel out the human. We really can pray, 'Give us this day our daily bread.'

LENT 5

In God's time

> St. John 8. 59 (NEB) *'They picked up stones to throw at him, but Jesus was not to be seen; and he left the temple.'*

No, it did not happen. There was no crumpled form of Jesus on the stone-flagged floor of the Jerusalem temple. No hasty covering of a bloodstained, bruised and broken body, battered with stones and hustled out to burial. It did not happen. There were stones there, everywhere stones, because the temple was still in process of building, and the Jews actually lifted them, but no stoning took place. Jesus did not die with stones. Had this happened there would have been no cross, no place, no instrument of death capable of acting as a symbol. The cross came. In God's time it came. And that is how Jesus looked on death. That is how he looked on the bending bodies and elevated arms. These ugly signs did not necessarily portray death. Nor did that attempt early on, back in Nazareth, to crowd him over the cliff. Death will only come in God's time. 'They picked up stones to throw at him, but Jesus was not to be seen; and he left the temple.'

Do we think like that about death? Do we believe like that? And you say there is no need to think about it at all. That is what everyone says, but the fact remains, we do think. We can scarcely not think. For all the advances of medical science this century in saving life, we are all closer to sudden death than ever before. You only have to be absent-minded for a second in Victoria Grove during the rush hour, or almost any hour, and step off the pavement, and life will be over. In Britain every year thousands of lives get suddenly snatched away by the agency of the motor-car. We take it as the price demanded by the modern god of mobility. We take our lives in our hands. Or do we believe they are in God's hands? Death will only be in God's time, and will only be as God intended.

It is arresting to see how thoughts like this probe our faith. Is ours a lively faith? Is it effective? Does it make any difference to practical living? What differences can faith make?

One of the *first* accomplishments of faith is liberation.

We are told in the scriptures of certain men who all their lifetime, through fear of death, were subject to bondage. That was never true of Christ. He knew he would die, of course. Was there any life more precarious than Christ's, from the moment he began to preach, from the moment he challenged the *status quo*, from the moment he uncovered the lies, subterfuges and hypocrisy that engineered the society of his day. Men picked up stones to throw at him. But he was never in bondage through fear of death, never dogged, dwarfed nor depressed by death. Jesus was a liberated man, liberated by his faith, that things only happen in God's time.

A *second* accomplishment of faith is action. Liberation, of course, leads to action, just as bondage restricts it.

In this, too, Jesus was astonishing. He did what he willed.

He said what he willed. Some of us, most of us set a watch before our lips for all but the most platitudinous sentiments. Not so Jesus. No, not even though men picked up stones to throw at him. He called his opponents sons of the devil, who is the father of lies. To read between the lines of today's Gospel is astonishing. Jesus' unbelievable thrust in argument. His unguarded phrases, his all but taunting with words likely to be banded about as blasphemy. But Jesus felt himself free to act, free to speak. Was not his life in the Father's hands? It was this faith that liberated him for action. And may it not be true that the Church is almost everywhere fighting a rearguard action today, if fighting at all, because her faith is weak. We do not actively believe we are in the hollow of God's hand. We do not reckon with a divine holding of the issues of life. We do not think events only happen in God's time. We see only our opponents picking up stones. We have forgotten that there is a victory that overcomes, and that is our faith.

Faith liberates. Faith calls for action. What else does faith accomplish? It makes us *see people in the right perspective*.

Think of Jesus. No official training in the Rabbinic schools. No degree. No recognition. Nothing, only his faith. How his opponents taunted him with being, as they put it, 'unlearned.' And yet he confronted them in dialectal argument and won. Jesus was not crushed by officialdom, not intimidated by badges, not put out by authority. Jesus was never 'put out.' He read through people with the clear eye of faith, the faith that truth actually exists, and can be known and recognized. Jesus, by means of faith in God, saw men as men. And though they picked up stones to throw at him, it was God who really controlled the issue of action. Faith makes for courage, clearsighted, cool courage. It is a probe to our faith how much of this we ourselves possess.

What an unusual picture the Gospel for today puts out on view! Jesus as a controversialist. Controversy is not an activity we like today to associate with religion. There are times for getting together. The Pope meets an Archbishop.

Thank God for that. The Anglicans hold conversations with the Methodists, and conversations with the Presbyterians. Thank God for all these dialogues. We want no bigotry. No intolerance. But the fifth Sunday after Lent descends to the cellar to bring up this picture of Christ as a controversialist, and we gaze in amazement. Words hurled backwards and forwards. Charges and counter-charges. Tempers rising. And look! Men actually picking up stones to cast at Jesus for what he said. Not outsiders, but insiders, priests and lawyers, teachers of the people. Take it away, take that picture back to the cellar, stow it in the basement of the Christian collection of dominical paintings. Or has it something, perhaps to say, we ought to hear? Be careful you do not tolerate everything. The Church, through fear of having stones thrown, might come to the point of tolerating anything. Believe what you like. Practise what you like, worship how you like, all in the name of toleration! But that is not what our master did. He spoke and he acted though men picked up stones to throw at him. He contended for the faith.

What is our faith like? Is it something for which we should contend? If it is something that gives us liberty, action and perception, surely it is. And if it is something which enables us to believe that all events are in God's hands and God's time, we shall be following in the steps of our Master, who was not afraid when his opponents took up stones to throw at him; he trusted still in God.

PALM SUNDAY

A woman of society

> St. Matthew 27. 19 *'Have thou nothing to do with that just man: for I have suffered many things this day in a dream because of him.'*

INTRODUCTION

Very often Scotland Yard is puzzled how to discover the perpetrator of some horrible crime. In these days in which we live in a capital city, this is all too frequent an occurrence. There is so little evidence, so little to 'go upon.' And then, perhaps, half an envelope is found near the scene of the crime. Nothing more. But there is writing on it. Half the stamp is visible, and the franking by the post office. From that tiny piece of evidence, and nothing else, the whole case gets built up and the criminal caught and brought to justice.

Today I bring to your notice one tiny scrap of information about a woman. It is all we have, nothing more, only one verse from the gospel of St. Matthew in the Gospel for today, but from it we can build up a clear picture of what this woman was, and perhaps even draw a lesson for ourselves. The verse is, 'Have thou nothing to do with that just man: for I have suffered many things this day in a dream because of him.'

1. *The Story*

This is Pilate's wife speaking. Pilate the Procurator, the man who found Jesus innocent, and tried to let him off, but dare not. First of all, you note *she was in Jerusalem*. Not all wives of Roman officers accompanied their husbands to Jerusalem. Very few, indeed, would accompany them during Passover week. Rome was far more pleasant, far more fun, perhaps even more pleasant, and more fun when your husband was away. And Jerusalem was fanatical. The Jews were fanatical. There was only needed the slightest provocation, and off would start a riot, a religious riot, and then someone might be killed. It might be yourself. But the Lady Claudia Procula *came* to Jerusalem with her husband in Passover week. What does that tell you about her? She cared for this man. She shared the worries of government with this man. There was nothing that troubled him, kept him awake at nights, wore him down by its weight, she did not know. Pontius Pilate possessed one of life's most valuable assets, a woman's love, sufficiently unselfish to share the hazards of his office.

2. *What else do we know about her?*

She was a heathen woman. Not heathen in the sense of uncultured, my guess is she was highly sophisticated, well known in Roman society, possessed of all the arts and graces of her upper class, but she was an outsider to the Israel of God, she did not belong. The Romans had no real religion, no idea of a personal God, no notion of God ever acting for men. The Lady Claudia Procula had no faith of this kind at all.

3. *Something happened*

She found herself in Jerusalem. And in that last week you could not move in the city without being reminded of Jesus of Nazareth. You turned a corner, and your chariot could not proceed till a way was cleared, because of the crowds listening to him preaching. You could not overhear some snippets of conversation in the bazaar, but what it was about Jesus of Nazareth. Either he had healed someone, or restored peace of mind to someone, or he had floored the Pharisees in argument, those pernickety men who made life so difficult for her husband. And when her maid came in to do her hair, that Jewish girl with her sallow face and large brown eyes, it was always Jesus she talked about, Jesus. Did her ladyship think they would kill him? Would the Galileans perhaps rise up to protect him? They were mad about him; he was their prophet. Oh madam, you should have seen him last Sunday on the roadway leading to the city! Palm branches cut down from the trees! Garments torn off and thrown down on the roadway! Oh, you should have seen him, sitting on that donkey, mounted like a king. Oh, my lady, he is lovely, so young, so strong, so kind, so good. Do you think they will kill him? Oh, my lady!

And the Lady Claudia Procula, who shared all her husband's worries, had known for weeks past how runners kept on running into the Governor's headquarters. Nobody moved in Judaea, no one preached in Galilee, but a report went back to the Government department in Jerusalem, or down to Caesarea. All that could be known of Jesus was known in the palace. Pilate knew it. And at nights, after dinner, when the candles were burning low, and the servants had removed themselves at last, Pilate's wife would gently ask, 'Tell me, husband, what is the latest about this Jesus of Nazareth? What does he look like?'

Did she ever see him? Did she perhaps one day borrow her hairdresser's cloak, and slip out into the streets to the back of some crowd, to watch Jesus' face, and to listen to that voice? I think so. She saw those fingers, sensitive fingers, hands strong as a workman's, but also so gentle; they healed people by touching. A woman notices hands.

4. *The dawn*

She lay on her couch, Roman fashion. She hadn't slept all night. And now he was out there in the guardroom, that frightening place of probing questions, and Jesus and her man out there face to face with each other. And she could not be present. . . .

But all that night she had dreamed. What it was we do not know; some writing on the wall, some writing on a cross. . . . Oh, surely it could never be, *that* body on a cross, those hands pierced with nails. . . . If that is what she dreamt, I can understand her words, 'I have suffered many things this day in a dream because of him.'

CONCLUSION

What does it all add up to? Not much, you say. A woman goes crazy over a young preacher? We've heard all that before.

A woman who rises no higher than telling her husband to lay off Jesus because punishment of him upsets her beauty sleep.

(*a*) But I ask you, notice this morning what Jesus himself said, that he who is not against me is for me. Could charity be more broad than that? Christ counts as his own all those who do not stand in open opposition.

(*b*) I also ask you to take seriously the idea that Pilate's wife became a Christian, for I cannot think that her spiritual pilgrimage ended in a nasty dream. No, she went on finding out more and more about Jesus, till she became a firm believer, one of the saints in Caesar's household of whom Paul spoke. And I shall go on wondering if Pilate himself—I know all the legends about him—I shall go on wondering if she didn't, by her faith, bring peace of mind even to her husband, at last, about the terrible mistake he made upon the judgement seat, when he condemned the Christ to crucifixion.

APPLICATION

This is the lesson of the Lady Claudia Procula, wife of Pontius Pilate; it doesn't matter where our faith begins, even in some sentimental attraction for a preacher. The test is, does it go on from there, on to seeking the defence of Christ, on to a personal belief in him, and trust in him, on to trying to minister him and his Gospel to your own family and society. There is no-one, of whatever section of society, who cannot find in Christ their peace. A common criminal found it, crucified with Jesus; so also did the Lady Claudia Procula in the Governor's palace; at least, she began to find, from that day onward, that faith in Christ could meet her deep-down need no Roman society nor paganism could touch.

And that is still true today, here in the West End of London. We can find satisfaction about the destiny of life as we commit ourselves to Christ and his cross. It is what our last hymn is about. We shall sing to renew our dedication. It is, 'When I survey the wondrous cross.'

GOOD FRIDAY

An advertisement

St. Mark 15. 26 *'And the superscription of his accusation was written over,* THE KING OF THE JEWS.'

INTRODUCTION

I am afraid it was an advertisement. I mean that caption of Pilate's. I put it like that because advertisement can be vulgar. It is vulgar to exhibit in public what should only be experienced in private. Birth and death belong to that category. And here was Jesus dying in public. And as if that wasn't enough, this caption, put there in the first place as a snub to Jewry, 'And the superscription of his accusation was written over, "THE KING OF THE JEWS."'

But the advertisement had to be, that is the awful thought. Had Jesus been crowded over the cliff at Nazareth, as he nearly was, there would have been no cross, no symbol, nothing that makes an advertisement of the love of God, and the sin of men. And the same would have been true had he been stoned in Jerusalem, as he nearly was in Passover week, or been knifed in some dark street at night, and his body tossed over the city wall. That is why Jesus did not reside in Jerusalem at night during Passover week, but out in Bethany. There had to be advertisement in his death; and the price was vulgarity, a naked body beaten almost to a pulp, that ridiculous crown of thorns, and, to top it all, that caption meant to snub, 'And the superscription of his accusation was written over, "THE KING OF THE JEWS."'

But what does it advertise? I mean that snubbing caption Pilate wrote. It advertises the kingly life of Christ. It advertises the sobering fact that men kill what is kingly, and thirdly, it advertises the fact that the kingliness lives on, and that spells hope.

1. *The caption advertises the kingly life of Christ*

Was Jesus a king, then? Even Pilate asked that question, and Jesus answered, 'You say I am.' Yes, that was it. Even Pilate could believe it. Everyone who met him could believe it. Jesus was a king. A king of the art of living; a kingly man though bound with chains; a king, though reared in poor surroundings. There was no fumbling on his part. No cringing. No obsequiousness. No defeats by depression. Always with steady step he walked, come what may, straight towards his goal with a kindly word to all along the road.

2. *We crucified him*

That is what the caption also advertises. 'The superscription of his *accusation* was written over.' The thing Jesus had done wrong, from our point of view, was to live in the world under *our* conditions, with only *our* faith, *our* flesh, *our* environment at his disposal. The thing Jesus had done wrong was to live the kingly life with our materials. So we crucified him.

It is not an attractive advertisement. It is, in fact, most unattractive, because it advertises the nasty twist in so much human nature. Go to some of these new flats being erected here in Kensington. Look at those lifts as I have done. Brand new things, all lined with lovely polished wood. But within days of their erection they were scored across in many places by irremovable deep and ugly knife-marks. And if you say this kind of shabbiness does not belong to cultured people, let me remind you how some writers, gifted with the art of words, never put pen down on paper except to denigrate the reputation of the great.

That is what the crucifixion was. Man's denigration of the kingly life. A terrible advertisement. The flogging. The dressing up. That crown of thorns. The cross designed to drag all dignity away. Nakedness in public. Death drawn out till the final dregs. That is how men tried to rid our world of the embarrassment of goodness. 'And the superscription of his *accusation* was written over, "THE KING OF THE JEWS."'

3. *The kingliness remains*

The caption is also the advertisement of that. I will ask you to notice that it was of the humiliated, writhing, zig-zag pain-contorted Jesus, the dying criminal, crucified beside him, said, 'Jesus, remember me when thou comest into thy kingdom.' He recognized the kingship still. And it was of that battered remnant, limp upon the bloodstained wood, that the Roman in charge of the humiliation confessed, 'Truly, this was a Son of God.'

Kingliness of life is something no cruelty can destroy. Goodness is something no sin of man can ever do away. Purity is eternal. It lasts for ever. It outlives all the battering, defaming, jeering and victimization that has gone on since the world began, and goes on still in London now. It is the ribald laughter which looks shabby in the shadow of Christ's cross.

Not his patience, not his unabusive tongue, not the whispering of his prayers for strength, not his commendation of his mother. These things shine at Calvary with a golden radiance, the only radiance there. This is the third truth the caption on the cross is there to advertise, that when all the leering, lewdness, cruelty and filth have disgorged their worst, the kingliness of life shines on.

CONCLUSION

That is where I find hope at the cross. That is why it is for me a shining, golden thing. It tells me rottenness is not the final commentary on life. Good will triumph in the end. Such is the advertisement set up upon that ugly hill outside a city wall. And when on Easter morning the sun climbs up above the skyline, it lights upon that cross and makes it look the shining thing it is. Not even death can defeat goodness. It will live on through this to another world, and so will all those countless men and women who dare to stand in faith beside the crucified, and acknowledge him as King.

EASTER DAY

The new dimension

St. John 20. 1 (PBV) '*The first day of the week cometh Mary Magdalen early, when it was yet dark, unto the sepulchre....*'

INTRODUCTION

Why did she do that? It's a long story, and I can't tell it all; but if I tell you a little, I think you'll understand, that is, if you understand the human heart at all.

For years, I admit, I have been against identifying Mary Magdalene with the Mary who anointed Jesus' feet, the Mary who lived at Bethany, wept over the loss of her brother, and the Mary who broke the alabaster box of ointment. I see now there is as much for the identification as there is against. So with Archbishop Temple I shall decide *for*, in which case I can piece together her story.

The Story

Mary lived in Magdala, a little town on the western shore of the lake of Galilee, notable for dyestuffs. It was a rich town, so rich its tribute had to be carried away in wagons; but it was an evil place, so evil that according to the Talmud it was subsequently destroyed for harlotry.

Perhaps, then, we can guess at Mary's life. The early part is only a guess. Occupying troops making for Magdala. But Mary was not for purchase. Then there came one soldier, so different, so kind, so strong. Yes, she would marry him. Her brother Lazarus and her sister Martha remonstrated, of course. They remonstrated for hours. But Mary would do it. She married her man from Italy. It was like a French girl marrying a German officer in the war. And then, of course, it happened. The troops moved on, back to Italy. Would he take her to Italy? A Jewish girl in Rome? What would they say there about a Hebrew girl! She wasn't even rich by Roman standards. So the day came. The terrible 'goodbye.' The Italian swinging along the road with the singing, marching legions. Maybe he left her a present.[1] Something to remind her of him. A pound of oil of spikenard, very precious, in a lovely alabaster box. She covered it with tears as the singing died away, and the tramping of the marching legions. All she had left now of her marriage was a box, and the memory of the tramping legions, tramping back to Rome.

Her family, I am afraid, let it be known that they had told her so. She felt outcast, outraged, outside any further regard by anyone at all. What mattered if she threw her life away? She would drown it in utter, reckless and complete abandon. It was easy in Magdala with another lot of troops nearby. Easy Mary, they call her. Decent people whispered, 'She must have seven devils.'

---

[1] For this suggestion I am indebted to Clarence May, *Before the Cross and After* (Faith Press, 1966), p. 13.—Author.

Then one day there came 'another man,' a man who asked for nothing. A man who somehow made you feel your worst in his presence, and, at the same time, your best in his presence. And he forgave her what she'd done. No-one else did. Not the synagogue. Not her family. But this man did. There was no need to tell her she was wrong. She knew she was wrong. But he seemed to understand. It made her a new woman. She left the nameless life completely, and for ever. And, one day, seeing him reclining in a Pharisee's house, she slipped in, touching his feet, and before she could recover herself, burst into tears, which fell on his feet, tears of gratitude for restoration.

And it was a new life. She became a disciple of the man Jesus. She was in the company which followed him throughout Judaea and Galilee. He even came to her reunited home in Bethany. She listened to his teaching, drinking it in, even to the extent of irritating her sister.

And when the day broke on which Jesus let it be known that he would soon be taken away, she sensed the situation. She knew about partings, and all their hurting poignancy. Then she brought out the alabaster box, the box of oil of spikenard, a pound's weight, very precious, and poured its contents, every ounce, over his feet. The breaking of the box meant the breaking of the old life that brought her such unhappiness.

Then they caught him, who had done no wrong, but only good. The Jews caught him. The Romans caught him. Troops from Italy. They marched him away, not to Italy, to Calvary, to a cross, to crucifixion, the man who had brought her back from hell. They killed him, slowly, cruelly, spitefully. They killed him. Mary of Magdala saw it all. She was there as close as she could be. She saw it to the bitter end. Perhaps her tears fell again upon his feet, crucified feet on a blood-stained cross, and she wiped them with her hair.

So I come to my text, 'The first day of the week cometh Mary Magdalen early, when it was yet dark, unto the sepulchre.' I began by asking why she came. Need I ask now?

And what did she find? Not what she expected. The narrative (it is the Gospel for today), goes on, 'and findeth the stone taken away from the sepulchre.' It was the beginning of her introduction to a new dimension. She thought she was to pay her final tributes to a man that was dead. The truth, however, was that she was entering a new stage of spiritual experience, a higher stage, a stage of devotion not governed by attachment to a physical form, and blown along by sentiment, but an awakening of her spirit to a divine presence.

CONCLUSION

Let me end with a question. What is real Christian religion?

Real Christian religion is breaking away from all we know to be unworthy in the presence of Christ.

Real Christian religion is reverence for the man, Jesus of Nazareth, all he said, all he taught, all he was in himself.

Real Christian religion, however, is more than both those attitudes tied together. It is experience of a new dimension. It is believing that Christ is with us now, beyond his death, beyond *our* death; beyond everything, and anything that would shut him out—time, space, circumstance, calamity, sin or misfortune. Christ is with us still, the victorious, the understanding, the human. It is God over all and in all, he is with us still.

EASTER 1

Life of a different quality

St. John 20. 19 (NEB) *'Late that Sunday evening, when the disciples were together behind locked doors, for fear of the Jews, Jesus came and stood among them.'*

INTRODUCTION

I don't know whether you believe this or not? I don't know if you believe John was sitting there, and James, and perhaps Andrew in the corner, and Philip, and all the other apostles....

There was a great key turned in the lock, perhaps a bar across the door as well, and all the shutters on the windows screwed into their positions. You would take all those precautions if you had seen your Lord and master crucified, and wonder if your turn was coming next. Then, without any opening of those doors or shutters, there is the man they crucified, standing in the midst.

1. *Do you believe it?*

Supposing you do believe it, do you reckon this story has been preserved simply because this strange event took place in some room no longer traceable in ancient Jerusalem? No, the story is told because what occurred there has happened time and time again since. All these stories in the Bible are true because they keep on happening. What we have here is existential truth.

Now I agree, of course, that with our twentieth-century outlook, belief in miracles is a struggle. *I* have to struggle. But the situation isn't too bad if you keep all the miracles shut away between the covers of the Bible. Then we can be like Peter, who blurted out after Christ's resurrection, 'I am going fishing.' Big things happened in the past, maybe. Who knows? But they don't happen now. Better get on with the routine jobs. That is all there is for us. 'I am going fishing, I am going to get my car serviced, I am walking to Knightsbridge to buy a new spring outfit.' But what the New Testament story says is that, when Peter went fishing, he was confronted by the risen Christ on the shore. It is like seeing Christ in Harrod's. This is the point of the fourth Gospel, as distinct from the Synoptic Gospels, as every student of the New Testament knows, it is the record of spiritual experience now, that is why it is true.

So this is the question for 1966, concerning my text about Christ appearing within a locked room, not, did it happen in A.D. 29, but, does it happen now? Is the account a true account of contemporary experience?

2. *A desire to believe*

And someone says, 'I'd like to believe it, but I can't, I would need positive and concrete evidence.' And then you read only a few verses farther on, and there is Thomas taking the words out of your mouth, 'And unless I see the mark of the nails.... unless I put my finger where the nails were... I will not believe.' It is all true, isn't it? As I said, true to life; true to your life.

And make no mistake, half of us would like to believe. We would like to believe bolts and bars do not have the final word in life, we would like to believe that the doctor's verdict on an illness may not be final, we would like to believe that materialism is not life's ultimate answer. Like to believe that if the universe is pliable in the scientist's hands, it must be more pliable, and even safer in God's hands; like to believe that D. H. Lawrence was wrong when he wrote in a postscript to Katherine Mansfield: 'Don't worry, Kate, Jesus is a back number.' We would like to believe that God can work miracles in his universe.

3. *Afraid of the idea*

But the other half of us is afraid of the idea. It's all a bit too much. It brings you up face to face with life of a different quality. It won't let you settle down behind conventional fences, phrases and clichés. It won't argue that money settles everything. It won't think only in terms of human brains and brawn; there are divine possibilities. We are half afraid of it. Life is safer with the conventional, more predictable, more comfortable.

CONCLUSION

And so, on this first Sunday after Easter, we stand uneasily before this picture of Christ entering in among the fear-stricken disciples. We are not sure we like it. The conventional Church is not sure that it likes it. If it is very radical it won't even concede that it represents historical truth. If it is very stupid, it will think to escape the difficulty by calling it existential truth, which it is. But the truth still probes. It is like a masterpiece in an art gallery. It judges us. It asks if we want to believe in a God who does things now, in a Christ who is an ever-present reality? The Cardinal Archbishop of Westminster put the point well, at the United Service of Witness in his cathedral on Good Friday—'We are reverencing one who died because he is not dead.'

One way of affirming our will to believe is in the Holy Communion. The service depends on the Resurrection. It affirms a real presence, a divine presence ready to break through to us now, gathered together like the disciples in the upper room those centuries ago. When Christ comes, he never leaves us as we were before. The necessity is to get beyond the point of disturbance to the settled conviction of trust in him. Then life of a new quality begins, eternal life, life with different eyes. That is what Christ brings; and that is why the disciples, after the Resurrection, were different from what they were before. They knew materialism is not the explanation of our world.

EASTER 2

The pattern

St. John 10. 11 *'I am the Good Shepherd.'*

INTRODUCTION

The priest is up for examination today, not that a process of detraction may be embarked upon, that is never Christian, but a process of prayer. The priest needs praying for, that he may live up to his stiff pattern. What is it? It is presented in the picture given of Christ in today's Gospel.

1. *The pattern speaks of the good shepherd*

The Greek word for good means 'attractive.' We might sentimentalize this, and conjure up pictures of a loving man caressing tender lambs. Such action played little part in the life of an eastern shepherd, or any shepherd. The good shepherd was strong, efficient and wise. He could drive away prowling beasts, rescue a sheep fallen down a gully, and sense where fresh pastures might be. The Christian priest is to be attractive by reason of his capability. People are attracted by someone who is strong.

2. *The pattern speaks of the shepherd giving his life for the sheep*
It is the sheep that concern him first, not himself. On this Sunday the priest has to examine himself, to see if he is 'spending himself' in the ministry.

> Go, labour on; spend, and be spent,
> Thy joy to do the Father's will;
> It is the way the master went;
> Should not the servant tread it still?
>
> H. BONAR, 1808-89

3. *The pattern speaks of the shepherd knowing his sheep*
This is not difficult when the flock is small, yet the difficulty of *really* knowing people always remains. The worst situation is when a priest sees people as merely making up 'communion totals.' The pattern today requires that the priest shall know each pair of hands outstretched to receive the sacred elements. Into *those* hands, the hands of the person he knows, he places the bread.

'The body of our Lord Jesus Christ, which was given for THEE. . . .'

APPLICATION

You should pray for your parish priest, that he may follow this pattern. There is no better prayer you could pray for your parish, than so to pray for him.

EASTER 3
New birth

INTRODUCTION

What a thrill there is when a new baby arrives, that is, of course, if the baby is wanted. Joy fills the mother's heart. Anxiety and the memory of pain rapidly fade away.

Perhaps Jesus was describing what took place in his own home in Nazareth. Perhaps the woman mentioned in today's Gospel—'A woman, when she is in travail, hath sorrow, because her hour is come: but as soon as she is delivered of the child, she remembereth no more the anguish, for joy that a man is born into the world'—was Mary herself.

1. *Rejoicing lies on the other side of birth*

That is the joy the disciples of Jesus would experience. Not birth into this life, that had taken place; not birth into the world to come, that was not yet; but a birth destined to occur in about six weeks from the Lord's death and resurrection. The new birth in the Spirit.

2. *Christian joy cannot exist without Christian rebirth in the Spirit*

Without it there exists only struggling, failure and ineffectiveness. Such was the disciples' experience. They misunderstood Jesus. They forsook Jesus. Peter, the chief disciple, even denied Jesus. But all that changed at Pentecost. The disciples became marked for their buoyancy.

3. *How does the new birth take place?*

The writer of the fourth Gospel, from which today's reading is taken, makes it quite plain in the third chapter. It takes place by the action of God's spirit when a man looks steadfastly at the cross and accepts the crucified Christ as his ultimate security. Then he is a new man. He is reborn into a new sphere. He sees Jesus again. In a sense he sees him for the first time. He sees him as the Christ, the Lord of life, the Saviour. And in that fresh seeing, joy comes. It is about this that the Gospel for today speaks.

EASTER 4

The interpreter

St. John 16. 15 *'He shall receive of mine, and shall show it unto you.'*

INTRODUCTION

In our drawing-room at home we have a small reproduction of Pieter de Hooch's 'Boy with the Pomegranates.' I bought it several years ago, because I have long been attracted to the Dutch school painting. Although, however, I have looked at that picture for a long time, I had never really seen it until the other day, when its detail was shown to me by the speaker in the popular broadcast, 'The Picture of the Month.' He spoke of 'The Boy with the Pomegranates.' I was quite amazed at what there was to be seen, and what I, in fact, have seen ever since.

Two disciples of Christ had this experience at another level, on the road to Emmaus on Easter Day. The risen Christ took the scriptures and showed them things they had never seen, but which were there, the things concerning himself. It was a heart-burning experience.

The possibility for us now is that the Holy Spirit of God will join us on the journey of life, and be an interpreter to us. He will take the things of Christ and show them unto us. There are, however, certain preliminaries which are necessary.

1. *There has to be something to interpret*

First, I needed to have my Pieter de Hooch, even if only in a cheap reproduction, if the broadcast interpretation about the painting was to mean anything to me. We must have a Bible in our spiritual life, we must have knowledge of its contents, and especially of Christ himself, if the Spirit of God is to interpret life to us with meaning. The Spirit of God does not work in a vacuum, he takes the things of Christ.

2. *We need the Spirit's interpretation*

Religion does not consist simply of religious knowledge. The disciples on the Emmaus road knew the scriptures, but they did not know the interpreted scriptures. What the Spirit does is to show the scriptures *unto us*. Then we do not only see, for example, a paralytic in Capernaum, we see ourselves as that paralytic, unable to walk in faith through life, but needing Christ's word of healing.

3. *Prayer*

Before, then, we read the scriptures, hear the Gospel, or expose ourselves to the ministry of the word, *we should pray to the Holy Spirit*, the illuminator, the interpreter. 'Holy Spirit of God, open my eyes, that I may see, may see myself, may see thyself in thy word, and in thy world, to thy glory. Amen.'

CONCLUSION

Have the things of Christ been interpreted to us? Is it that we do not know the things of Christ? Is it that we think we know the things of Christ? Is it that we have never asked the *Spirit* of Christ to make them real to us? There is no room for vagueness or self-sufficiency in things pertaining to God.

EASTER 5

Buoyancy

St. John 16. 33 *'Be of good cheer; I have overcome the world.'*

1. *Early Christian buoyancy*

On May 31st, 1578, a man digging for pozzolana in a vineyard near the Via Salaria (just outside Rome) broke into a tunnel, and found himself in a world of the dead. He saw a narrow, rock-hewn passage lined on each side with tomb niches, and as he ventured inside, he found the gallery to be intersected with others, leading on into a labyrinth. This discovery amazed Rome. The men of that time (the sixteenth century) were more excited by the thought that a city of the dead existed, unsuspected, beneath their feet, than by the fresh and beautiful world of early Christianity, which had emerged after its long entombment. So writes H. V. Morton, in *A Traveller in Rome*. And had they known then what Father Marchi had told us now, that possibly six million Christians have been buried in these tombs, and that if you placed all the galleries end to end, they would extend for 600 miles, they would have been dumbfounded, as indeed we almost are, at the thought of all this, down below the ground still, just beyond the walls of Rome.

It is still possible, of course, to go down into that gaunt cradle of our faith, and of civilization. You can see the words on the tombs, recognize the Greek letters which stand for Christ, and the drawings of the fish which was the Christian 'password.' There are paintings, too, on some of the niches, not great works of art this time, not Raphael, Michelangelo or Botticelli, but paintings by ordinary folk, who came down with a brush and a pot of paint to cover the resting-place of their loved one with little drawings of flowers, trees and other homely scenes, perhaps things the deceased had loved.

In these underground passages you can hear again the voices of the first Christians; and the message they give is one of faith, hope and charity. Everywhere you see on the tombs the words 'Rest' and 'Sleep.' There never is the hopeless word 'Vale,' 'Farewell,' which sighs its way through all the pagan cemeteries, but 'Vivas in Deo' and 'In pace Christi.' A girl is called by her parents, 'Sweet as honey,' and husbands and wives describe each other in terms of affectionate gratitude. And this is what Morton says, in all the hundreds of miles of tunnels, not once is Christ pictured on the cross. The Christ of the catacombs is the good shepherd, a youthful, beardless figure in Greek dress, who might at first sight be Apollo or Orpheus. This is what comes down to us from these early Christians in Rome, millions of them, a great fragrance of joy, gratitude and confidence, even about death. These people in the midst of a pagan and cruel society really believed in Christ's Resurrection, and it gave them this buoyancy and peace which they have left in their burial grounds.

2. Christ's buoyancy

When we turn back to the life of Jesus, we find there was one word constantly on his lips. It was the word, 'Be of good cheer.' It is the final word in the Gospel for today, 'Be of good cheer, I have overcome the world.' It is a word which occurs seven times in the New Testament, and every one of those usages is connected with Jesus.

There was Jesus saying to the paralysed man, 'Son, be of good cheer, thy sins are forgiven.' And to the woman with a haemorrhage, 'Daughter, be of good cheer, thy faith hath saved thee.' And to the disciples on the storm-tossed lake, as they see Christ coming towards them, 'Be of good cheer, it is I, be not afraid.' And when a blind man called out to Jesus for healing, the crowd said to him, 'Be of good cheer, he is calling you.' Yes, the word 'Be of good cheer' was characteristic of Jesus, so characteristic, that when Paul was in prison, he saw a vision of his Lord, and these are the words that came to him, 'Be of good cheer, for as you have testified concerning me at Jerusalem, so must you bear witness also at Rome.'

3. The Church's real security is buoyancy

In these days in which we are now living, when the Church is being attacked from all sides, and some of the attacks are directed towards very real weaknesses in our system, we are driven to ask where our real strength lies. Some, perhaps, think it resides in the successful financial investment policies of the Church Commissioners; others in the Establishment, that is, our connection with the State; and others look to our bishops in apostolic succession. These buttresses are real, and they exist. We can, perhaps, even thank God for them, but what in the end will commend the Church to mankind is not its securities, but its buoyancy. Men and women will only pay attention if Christians are different from an environment in which boredom, anxiety and envy play a very large part. By the presence or absence of buoyancy congregations will be judged. By this will be known whether or not we follow the Christ who said, the night before his crucifixion, 'Be of good cheer, I have overcome the world.' It involves entering into Christ's resurrection. This is where the Church, wherever it has been buoyant, has discovered its life, in the magnetic field of Easter Day.

SUNDAY after ASCENSION DAY
Forewarning

St. John 16. 1 (NEB) *'I have told you all this to guard you against the breakdown of your faith.'*

INTRODUCTION

Imagine a prisoner in a cell beyond the Iron Curtain, locked there for his faith. His captors try every means known to them to break down his faith: hunger, beatings, questionings far into the night, depressing information suggesting that all the churches have dwindled away in Europe, and all his relatives are dead.

In a very much lesser degree, all Christians are in that position today, under pressure to renounce their faith.

1. *The Church*

There is the pressure exerted by the anomalies, downright failures, and antiquarian customs of the Church. Christians wonder sometimes if it can survive, or have any future in the technological age.

2. *The Spirit of the Age*

There is the pressure exerted by the spirit of the age, which is hostile to any endurance of what is uncomfortable. There are strikes, resistance to any regulation of private morals, and a casting away of formality, especially in dress and manners. Only in certain physical spheres like mountaineering and pot-holing is endurance fashionable. But at its very heart the Christian faith places a willingness to put up with what we may not like. 'If any man would come after me, let him take up his cross and follow me.' The pressure of the spirit of the age is against this.

3. *Tragedy*

There is the pressure of life's illnesses and tragedies. That woman in full middle life, dying of cancer. Why? That Sunday School teacher who never recovered from the anaesthetic on the operating table. Why? *Does God care?* The pressure of events like this has always been a possible cause of the breakdown of faith.

CONCLUSION

Our Lord said, 'I have told you all this to guard you against the breakdown of your faith.' What had he told them? Two things.

First, his disciples must expect opposition. And this stands true, however up to date the Church becomes, or however buoyant. The people of non-faith will oppose.

Secondly, he has sent the Comforter, the strengthener. Technological and social progress has brought great gain, but crime, depression and envy march on apace. Life does not succeed unless the Spirit of Christ is present. That thought restores our shaky faith. Faith is necessary, after all. The Spirit of Christ is the strengthener. He helps us resist the pressures which might so easily lead to the breakdown of faith today.

WHITSUNDAY

The Church discloses the Spirit

> St. John 14. 22 (NEB) *'Lord, what can have happened, that you mean to disclose yourself to us alone and not to the world?'*

INTRODUCTION

That was Judas' question. Not Judas Iscariot, but the other Judas in the apostolic company, for two of them bore that name. It wasn't a silly question. It was a reasonable question. For weeks, months, even a year or two, Judas had been seen with Jesus, everywhere in Judaea and Galilee. And then in the upper room Jesus intimated that in future he would disclose himself only to his disciples, and not to the world. What could he mean? Would he perhaps work an astonishing miracle, and become invisible? Would he perhaps become an anchorite, making himself available only in his cell to his apostles?

We know now what Jesus meant. Judas Iscariot was already in mind, if not in act, on the way to betray Jesus. Death and Resurrection lay beyond for him. He could only be known, in future, by his disciples, because he could only be known by his spirit.

But is this still true? Is it true that Christ is only disclosed within the Christian group? Is isolation from the Christian Church out as far as all real understanding of Christ is concerned? The answer is 'Yes,' and that for three reasons.

1. *Christ's spirit*

It is not the body of Christ we encounter any more with our physical eyes and physical hands, but his spirit. A spirit, distinct from the human, belongs to a group. We talk of the spirit of a school, or of a ship's company. So Christ's spirit develops in the Christian group or church. Our Lord promised his spirit, not to an apostle in isolation, but to the company together in the Upper Room.

2. *Christ's spirit is encountered in a group*

The spirit we encounter is the spirit of the risen Christ, the living Christ, the spirit who is the life-giver. But life at the human level does not develop in isolation. It takes two people to produce life. A child living in isolation would be an idiot. The only thing we do alone is die. The opposite of death requires the opposite of isolation. The spirit of Christ, then, requires the group.

3. *Christ's spirit is revealed in the Christian community*

No one individual represents the body of Christ, but the whole Church. Not even one denomination, but all denominations. Individuals over-emphasize one aspect of Christ. The situation is like a distorting hall of mirrors. So it is that the spirit is disclosed only in the Christian community, and not to individuals in isolation.

APPLICATION

Is any one of us conscious of making little progress in our Christian development? Isolation could be our trouble. It is not possible to by-pass the Church and experience the disclosure of God's spirit. That spirit exists in all the world, but is manifested in the Christian company.

TRINITY SUNDAY

New life

St. John 3. 4 *'How can a man be born when he is old?'*

INTRODUCTION

We only need to change one word and we have a question on the lips of thousands today. 'How can a *Church* be born when it is old?' How can it gain new life, with its long history behind it?

A clear and decisive answer is given in the Gospel for today, clear, because it is set against a back-cloth of negatives.

1. *A church will* not *gain new life merely by the promotion of discussion*

Nicodemus met Jesus with the express purpose of promoting a discussion as between one rabbi and another. 'Rabbi, we know that thou art a teacher come from God....' But Jesus cut him short. 'Except a man be born anew, he cannot see the Kingdom of God.'

Is this what Christ would say to the modern Church seeking renewal? It will not come by talking, discussion, and the multiplication of conferences.

2. *A church will not gain new life merely by the provision of more and more information*

Nicodemus was a highly-informed member of his Church and of society. He also knew the skills in dialectal argument. Aware as he was, however, that he lacked something, Jesus did not provide yet more information.

Is this what Christ would say to the Church today, fed at every turn by statistics, reports and new theologies? More information will not furnish the renewal that is looked for.

3. *A church will not gain new life unless it understands the separation between flesh and spirit*

The shock in this story is that Nicodemus was at heart a materialist. A churchman, a preacher and a theologian, but basically a materialist! What conditioned everything in his view was the material, the natural and the human. 'How can a man be born when he is old?' To which Jesus replied, 'That which is born of the flesh is flesh; and that which is born of the spirit is spirit.' We believe in the natural. We must believe in the supernatural. But do we? Is not this our trouble?

CONCLUSION

What we need is to turn round and look in the opposite direction from the material, natural and human. Not because they are evil, but because there is another dimension. We must trust in the God who works miracles. He is known in Jesus, and experienced in the Spirit. Through trust in this Triune God, a new beginning takes place, the only adequate description for which is new birth.

TRINITY 1

Hell

St. Luke 16. 23 *'And in hell he lifted up his eyes, being in torments.'*

Close the book, brother! It is time we walked out. Of kindliness, of brotherliness, of sweet reasonableness, yes, and of the sacraments, we are willing to hear. But if you come in 1966 with any doctrine of judgement, retribution or hell, we must leave you. We are kindly people. We would not hurt a fly. Moreover, there is scarcely anything in our modern world we are not ready to forgive, condone, or explain away. Violence, fornication, stealing—the lot. Surely God cannot be less generous than man! No, we cannot hear this doctrine of hell. We are compelled to switch off, for the first Sunday after Trinity. Close the book, brother. It is time we walked out.

But the Church doesn't want you to walk out. So what does it do? It soft-pedals the doctrine. Its preachers do not preach about it. Who wants to be labelled a 'hell-fire' preacher, anyway? And from its tract cases and ecclesiastical manifestos, all such references are tacitly withdrawn. We go on as if hell didn't exist. And then Trinity 1 comes round. And this awkward passage of scripture we have to read. Not from some obscure part of the Old Testament, which we could easily explain away with a convenient doctrine of spiritual evolution, but a New Testament parable on the lips of Jesus. The story of the rich man and Lazarus. And in it, this hurting phrase, '. . . and in hell he lifted up his eyes, being in torments.'

What are we to think about hell? *First*, that it exists on the other side of death. There is a tendency now to be very free with our use of the word 'hell.' A man 'knocks hell' out of a tennis ball. A woman says her existence with her former husband was 'absolute hell.' A student describes some den he does not like as 'a hell of a place.' We keep the word as an adjective. It represents our ultimate description of extreme unhappiness. So we make it *this* worldly. Hell belongs to the here and now. And so, of course, there is an answer to hell.

It is to be sought in drugs, and to some extent in excessive alcohol. The absolute hell of the 1960s is to possess insufficient money for either drugs or alcohol. Then the only saviour is death, sometimes deliberately sought in suicide.

But what if death does not, after all, lead to annihilation? What if death is not a saviour? What if death is, in fact, a gate out of one form of existence into another, as modern psychical research suggests. Then it does not matter how loudly we may have trumpeted the idea that hell is not a place, but a state, it can be a state we take with us through the gate. So hell can have an *other* worldly reference. It can exist on the other side of death.

Which being so, of course, the torments are not physical. How could they be? Man has no physical body on the other side of death. Nor are there flames. How could there be? Matter, carbon and ignited gas do not belong to the spiritual existence on the other side of death. Nor need modern man bow to the pictures medieval man painted of the tortures of the after-life. Nor need he count them as everlasting, for time does not obtain in eternity. Perhaps Jean-Paul Sartre was nearer the mark when he wrote of the hell of human relationships gone wrong. And if you look in today's Gospel, that is what you will find hell to consist of, human relationships seen to be wrong, that cannot be put right. Today's *Epistle* is all about love, but in hell love cannot function. It burns, but it is sterile. Nothing happens. Nothing, therefore, is begotten. So it burns itself out. And the end is isolation, burnt out loneliness which goes on to nothingness, product of love sterility.

Secondly, the doctrine of hell is an interlocking stone in the arch of things the Christian Church believes. And suppose you knock it out. Suppose you say there is no retribution in the life to come for the wrongs committed in this life. What becomes of the *goodness* of God? Does God not bother if we behave rightly or wrongly? Is it all the same in the final wash? And if we say there is retribution in *this* life, what about the thousands who quite obviously 'get away with it,' and die peacefully in their beds. Are the great train robbers still at large suffering more than that poor engine-driver they knocked on the head, who was only doing his duty?

Suppose you do away with the doctrine of hell. For what purpose did God intervene in history? Why did the Incarnation take place? Why was Christ born in the crudities of a stable in Bethlehem? For our salvation, you say. But salvation from what? To save us from ourselves. To lift us up, and to point to a way of nobler living, till we are all positively overflowing with the milk of human kindness? But if this cosy humanitarianism was all God intended by his action, is not the crucifixion all too stark and stupid, a price unnecessarily high for something pretty cosy, anyway?

Doesn't it work out like this, that if you knock out hell, you'll have to knock out the goodness of God, the Incarnation, the Cross, and Resurrection, and half the other articles in the creeds as well. In fact, is not this what we see happening in the world today, a general crumbling of Christian beliefs?

This is my point. By all means let us think out carefully what we mean by hell, let us call it by its proper name, Hades; but if we knock it out just because fashion asks this of us, the laugh will be on the lips of our opposers. They want to see us crumbling.

Thirdly, we cannot abandon the doctrine of hell if we are to believe in the guidance of the Holy Spirit. Just think for a moment, Christ promised his Church the guidance of his Holy Spirit. It is reasonable that he should have done so. It would be *un*reasonable, had he founded it, and left it to its fate.

It is true, of course, the Church has made bad mistakes. Its ranks are composed of fallible and sinning man. But are we to suppose that a doctrine which has been held throughout its history, and one which is based on words from the lips of Christ himself, on more than one occasion, is utterly stupid, and not to be countenanced by intelligent people? If so, what are we to make of the doctrine of the Holy Spirit? What becomes of the spirit of truth in the Church? What of the truthfulness of Jesus?

This is my point. Examine, reface, readjust a stone in the arch of Christian doctrine if you like, but be careful how you knock it out, or you may find the whole arch in ruins at your feet.

But let me finish on another note. Jesus did not preach hell or hell-fire. He did not come to open the kingdom of hell for unbelievers. Behind the coming of Christ is the spacious love of God. 'God so loved the world, that he gave. . . .' But that love would be a sentimental, sloppy, stupid thing were it not set over against a real possibility of loss. God's love is acceptable because it appears as a costly rescue action. 'God so loved the world, that he gave his only begotten son, that whosoever believeth in him should not *perish* but have eternal life.' This is what the fourth Gospel says, the most spiritual of all four Gospels, the one that portrays experience of Christ now.

TRINITY 2

What is the Kingdom of God like?

St. Luke 14. 16 (NEB) *'A man was giving a big dinner party and had sent out many invitations.'*

INTRODUCTION

I wonder what you think the Kingdom of God is like. I wonder what the Jews thought it was like, in our Lord's day. Some kind of ecclesiastical government? Perhaps an endless church service! What do *we* think it is like? A serious thing? An occasion for wearing a black suit? How did Jesus represent the Kingdom of God? The Gospel for today tells us.

1. *The Kingdom of God is like a party*

'A man was giving a big dinner party and sent out many invitations.' Nor was this the only occasion when Jesus made this comparison. There was the parable of the ten girls. They were on their way to a wedding party. The Kingdom of God will be like that.

What picture do we give to the outsider of what the Kingdom of God is like? A thing of strain? Anxiety about liturgy? Uncertainty over bishops? Sometimes we give the impression that the Kingdom of God is a finance committee. What is wrong? Perhaps we haven't understood the Gospel!

2. *The Kingdom of God is like a party to which all the right people get invited first*

That is, the people you would expect to be there, the baptized, the confirmed, the married in church, the members of the Establishment. But they aren't all there. That is the shock. They are conspicuous for their absence where Christianity is a happy, easy, friendly sort of life. They offer excuses, most of them connected with work, except the one who got married (he was such a solemn fellow that he perhaps thought of his marriage as work!). The Church, however, *has* a certain priority in things pertaining to the Kingdom of God. This does not, however, mean that it need not bother to respond to Christ's invitation to partake of his kingdom.

3. *The Kingdom of God is like a party that is open to outsiders*

Think of it. Men coming in to dinner in open-neck shirts. The surprising thing is, outsiders want to come. They don't find the Kingdom of God a stuffy experience at all. What is more surprising, not all these people are morally upright. But the host wants them all in.

CONCLUSION

What impression does our Church give to outsiders, of what the Kingdom of heaven is like? Do they feel they are wanted?

TRINITY 3

Self-defence

St. Luke 15. 2 (NEB) ' "*This fellow,*" *they said, "welcomes sinners and eats with them.*" '

INTRODUCTION

Not many of us would like to try and put up a *defence* for an exclusive snobbish attitude to people. Jesus had to put up a defence for the reverse position. He mixed with all and sundry, even with people of doubtful reputations, the sort a churchman might be expected to avoid. His argument ran as follows.

1. *The inclusive attitude is reasonable*

'What man of you,' he says. It is an argument *ad hominem*. An argument which comes home to every reasonable human being. An argument which fastens on common practice. 'What man of you having a hundred sheep, if he lose one of them, doth not leave the ninety and nine in the wilderness, and go after that which is lost, until he find it?' You would expect a shepherd to want that sheep which has escaped out of the fold to be brought back and included among the others. It is impossible to think of him 'turning up his nose' and saying, 'I don't like that sheep, it is not my sort.'

2. *The inclusive attitude is normal*

Here is a woman possessing ten pieces of silver. They are strung together on a thread around her head. In our country it would be a necklace. Would it not be normal, if the thread broke and the silver pieces were scattered, for the woman to go on searching till she had *re*included even the tenth piece in the set? She would want to include them all. To exclude even one piece would not be normal.

3. *The inclusive attitude is the way of happiness*

There was widespread joy when the shepherd had included his hundredth sheep back in the fold. Joy among all the neighbours when the woman had tied in her tenth and final silver piece along with the others on her string. Inclusiveness produces inner satisfaction, exclusiveness inner dissatisfaction. The snob is not fundamentally a happy man.

CONCLUSION

Everything in Jesus' defence, however, depends on one point. The shepherd owned the sheep. The woman owned the coins. Because of that fact the missing sheep and the missing coin could both be described as 'lost.' The reason, therefore, why exclusiveness was unreasonable and abnormal for Jesus, was that he owned all the riff-raff of society as well as the respectable. He saw them as 'his people.'

The root cause of exclusiveness is a failure to appreciate how we belong to one another. It is Cain who first voices this in the bible, when he asks, 'Am I my brother's keeper?' We are responsible for our brothers. We belong to one another, all of us, which being the case, it is unreasonable, abnormal and unsatisfying to adopt an exclusive attitude to anyone.

TRINITY 4

Blind guides

> St. Luke 6. 39 *'Can the blind lead the blind? Shall they not both fall into the ditch?'*

INTRODUCTION

You don't know whether to laugh or cry. A blind man in an eastern street, taking the arm of another blind man to guide him. First, they all but collide with a load of furniture on the back of a donkey. Then they bump into a goat, to its evident surprise. Lastly, you see them making straight for an open ditch and, of course, they topple in. You see them remonstrating with each other in the muddy water at the bottom.

And God doesn't know whether to laugh or cry when he sees us, when he sees the Church, pontificating over conduct. We forget that we are blind.

What does the parable mean? the shortest Jesus told.

1. *The Church's job is not to moralize*

And if it is objected that this is the Church's job to lay down rules, and people are weak who do not speak up, it must be pointed out that the Church is compromised. Its eyes are not healthy. It cannot wholly see straight.

2. *The Church, however, must be discerning*

Even a blind man uses what faculties of hearing and feeling he possesses to find his way. So the Church, so the Christian man, must be discerning. There must be knowledge of what is going on, and the exercise of wisdom, but not condemnation.

3. *The Church's job is to present Christ*

He is not blind. He 'reads' people. He read the situation of the woman taken in adultery, and that of her accusers. He knows the springs of action.

CONCLUSION

In a changing world it is more important than ever for the Church to present Christ, and to make people *want* to carry out what they understand to be his will. This is the way not to 'fall into the ditch.'

TRINITY 5

Deep water

St. Luke 5. 4 (NEB) '*Put out into deep water and let down your nets for a catch.*'

INTRODUCTION

This is a command. It calls for obedience. This is the place where Christian discipleship begins. We obey an external authority. We obey the word of Christ.

1. *It is with obedience to authority that the modern world finds its greatest difficulty*

There is rebellion against the authority of the white races rebellion against all that smacks of the Establishment, rebellion against rules in morality, and Humanism is a revolt against imposed religious sanctions. In general, 'Jack is as good as his master.' The Christian life involves a struggle to come to the point of submission to the authority of Christ. Peter had to come to it. We all do.

2. *It was a command to put out into deep water*

Being a Christian does mean negotiating deep water. You can't touch bottom. You can't explain everything, not even the existence of God. This seems *very* deep water to people educated in the modern scientific method of weighing and measuring. We have to learn to appreciate a way of knowing, other than the scientific, the existential.

3. *Peter's act of obedience was justified*

He did as he was told. He put out into deep water. He let down the nets for a catch, and he got it, a tremendous haul. Note that the catch did not come first, and the obedience afterwards. Did Peter obey Christ because he saw something about him that evoked obedience? because he felt that Christ was concerned for him? because he sensed that in meeting Christ he was somehow meeting God? We do not know exactly why. Do we ever know *exactly* why we obey? But the act of obedience produced results. It put Peter on the Christian road.

APPLICATION

The Gospel for the fifth Sunday after Trinity could be calling us to abandon the shallow water of rationalism, or of mere empirical observation, for the deep water of obedience to the sovereignty of Christ. Response to this call could bring us greater riches in life than we thought possible. Everything depends on obedience in *faith*.

TRINITY 6

About anger

St. Matthew 5. 22 *'Whosoever is angry with his brother...'*

INTRODUCTION

I wonder what you would say, is anger a good thing, or is it a bad thing? Perhaps I might alter one word in my question to help you give an answer. Is *fire* a good thing, or is it a bad thing? It all depends, doesn't it, on whether the fire is in the right place, and whether it is under control? Last October we made careful plans to light up our furnaces in the church, so that the congregation should not feel the first pinch of winter's cold, decide our church was a cold place, and stay away in future. When, however, furnaces are first lit they smoke. Ours were so smoky some passer-by thought our church was on fire, telephoned the Fire Brigade, which promptly arrived and put out our fires with floods of water. But there was no need. The fire was in the right place. It was under control, and we very much wanted it, especially that week-end.

Anger is like a fire. It can be a bad thing, especially when misplaced and out of control. But it can be a good thing. St. Paul wrote in his letter to the Christians at Ephesus (4. 26. NEB): 'If you are angry, do not let anger lead you into sin....' There are times when anger is right, times when not to be angry would be quite wrong. He would be a downright evil man who could see a child being ill-treated, and not rise up in wrath. We read in the scriptures that sometimes God is angry. In the Gospel for today, however, we are warned of three ways in which anger can be wrong.

1. *It is wrong if it has no proper cause*

Jesus said, 'Whosoever is angry with his brother without a cause shall be in danger of the judgement.' We are given an instance of this in the story of the prodigal son. The elder brother was angry and would not go in when a festival of rejoicing was arranged for the return of the younger erring brother. This was anger based on injured pride. This, like resentment, is an insufficient cause. If we indulge in it we are in danger of the judgement. And judgement is a present process. It means we do our personalities positive harm this way.

2. *Anger destroys worship*

If you are angry with the vicar, another choir-man or someone who sits in the next aisle in the nave, it is better not to attend church that day. And even the collection is useless, because money given in worship represents self-oblation, and self-oblation is incompatible with anger. Reconciliation is the pre-requisite of worship. We have to be forgiving to our neighbours if we would receive in worship from the forgiving God. This is both psychological and theological truth.

3. *We must deal with anger quickly*

Anger may be right, but it is very dangerous if we harbour it. Far better to tackle your adversary furiously and be done with it, than to burn slowly in anger to him for days, weeks or (as we have heard) years. Anger is very like fire. You never know what harm it will do if you leave it alone and it gets out of control. The rule is, we must deal with anger quickly. 'Agree with thine adversary quickly,' said Jesus in the Sermon on the Mount from which today's Gospel is taken. Otherwise we may find ourselves in a position from which there is no return. Listen how St. Paul puts it: 'If you are angry, do not let anger lead you into sin; do not let sunset find you still nursing it; leave no loophole for the devil'; or, to put it in a nutshell, never go to bed angry.

CONCLUSION

All this is like a dentist's probe. We wince as we hear it. Perhaps we are angry at having to listen. Well, we had better get over it quickly. Obviously there must be trouble somewhere, or the probe would not hurt. We had better seek the Lord who is the healer, and what better place, what better time than in the sacrament today. And remember, it is a Communion service. We must be reconciled to one another there....

TRINITY 7
Man's wealth needs Christ

St. Mark 8. 4 *'From whence can a man satisfy these men with bread here in the wilderness?'*

INTRODUCTION

The straight answer, of course, is that it cannot be done. That is to say, not if the men are there, and the wilderness is there; which was precisely the situation when the disciples asked this question. Four thousand men at least had trailed across the countryside, full of expectancy, on the heels of Jesus. It is not easy to shake off *one* beggar. What do you do with four thousand? What do you do when you are concerned about their plight? And this was the situation that faced Jesus. 'I have compassion on the multitude, because they continue with me now three days, and have nothing to eat: and if I send them away fasting to their houses, they will faint by the way, for some of them have come from far.' So what Jesus did was to feed them, feed them with seven loaves and a few small fishes. And they were all satisfied, every one of them. There was food enough and to spare. The left over filled seven baskets.

Now it would be possible to reject this story outright, and I must confess, with good reason *if*, I say, *if* its purpose is to show Jesus as some kind of wonder worker. Man is unable to satisfy man with bread in a wilderness, but God can! But Christ did not act like a wonder worker. He did not produce loaves out of a hat. Bread did not come tumbling down out of heaven. And God never acts like that. A book has recently been published which prophesies starvation in the world by 1980. If that happens, people will die in Asia by the million.

God will not save them. My point is—if today's Gospel only says Christ is some kind of wonder worker, we can rightly reject it.

1. *Man has resources*

But look at the story more closely. When the disciples asked their hopeless question, 'From whence can a man satisfy these men with bread here in the wilderness?' Jesus said, 'How many loaves have *ye*?' Look and see what you possess yourselves.

This is the point. Man *is* able to feed men with bread in the wilderness, if he makes his resources available for all. In all this, the scientific humanists are right. Human ingenuity, scientific production methods, and the application of the mind to distribution, is able to meet the situation of world hunger. The big question, however, is, Will man do it? Will the resources of the earth, and the resources of the human brain be applied to meet the needs of man? Will they not be used simply to make more money? To keep up in the rat race for status? To provide more toys for our enjoyment? Are we sure, for instance, that the pouring out of millions of pounds on the moon projects is right? God knows what it has cost to inform us that stones on the moon's surface look exactly like stones in some gravel pit near the Great West Road. But America must do it, to keep up with the Russians. And we must be in on it to compete in communications, so that here in London we can see momentarily what they choose to show us in New York, and vice versa. But what if there is nothing worth showing! The first pictures that actually crossed the Atlantic in this way were of a night club! What a commentary! Please do not miss the point. The world possesses the resources, man possesses the brain to work marvels. The problem is, what marvels will he work? Will he feed the hungry in the wilderness? I will not answer the question, but only ask, where does all the foreign aid go in the underdeveloped countries that receive it? This is the point. When we complain of hunger, when we complain of a toppling £ sterling, God asks, what do you possess? The crisis is not one of materials, the crisis is not one of brains, the crisis is one of the human spirit, and its bitter, bitter poverty.

2. Man's resources need linking with Christ

'From whence can a man satisfy these men with bread here in the wilderness?' The answer is, by linking up human resources with the Spirit of Christ.

In the last decade or so we have become very superior about this kind of remark. I am not thinking now of the idea that human resources on their own are quite sufficient without Christ. I am thinking of the idea that we ought not to link love of God with material well-being. It is crude, selfish and unworthy. If we are to love God, we are to love him for himself alone. But are we? Is a man to love his wife for herself alone? Is he to say, 'Mary, dear, I am not in the least interested in all the things you do for me, looking after the house, providing meals, remembering my birthday, which I would otherwise forget myself, I only love you for yourself alone.' I know what would happen to Mary. She'd decide she wasn't loved at all! No! The time will come for us to talk about purely spiritual love when we are purely spiritual beings, and that time is not yet.

We must not resist then this idea, that committal to the Christ of God does mean the betterment of our material situation. Let one such illustration suffice. In a time of plenty, how many will profit if those who distribute that plenty are not honest men? This is what today's Gospel teaches. For all our resources of materials and brain power, the provision of the needs of men will not be forthcoming, unless the Spirit of Christ is present in the hearts of men. Our resources are sufficient only when they are linked with Christ's power over human motives.

3. Christ brings in a new dimension

But someone is unhappy at what I am saying. They sense rationalism. They want to cry out, 'But tell us, did it happen? Did Jesus feed 4,000 men with seven loaves in the wilderness, beyond the lake of Galilee?' Yes, I think so. I think there was a feeding of 5,000 or 4,000, perhaps both. I do not know. But I believe with all my heart, that Jesus is the Christ of God, and that wherever God is, we are in touch with another level of being than the human, the natural and the material, and then the possibilities of change are incalculable. This is what the story says. This is what the Gospel for today teaches.

APPLICATION

Here, then, is the lesson. *We cannot engineer our own safety.* Whatever assets we have, whatever moral assets, whatever material assets, whatever we think may be entered up in God's ledger, or our own, to our temporal and eternal credit, it does not add up to our safety, not to our country's safety, not to our individual safety. Without Christ, for all our loaves and fishes, we shall stay hungry men in the wilderness. Safety begins with looking to Christ, looking to him with those seven loaves in our hands. Looking to him with those seven good deeds in our memory. Without him they are just seven loaves that will go mouldy, seven good deeds that will turn sour in our consciousness. Without Christ we have no safety, temporal or eternal. It is the message we must proclaim today. Our wealth needs Christ if we are to profit by it. We cannot profit by our wealth alone.

TRINITY 8

The way of entry

> St. Matthew 7. 21 *'Not every one that saith unto me, Lord, Lord, shall enter into the Kingdom of heaven; but he that doeth the will of my Father which is in heaven.'*

Last summer, while in Portugal, I paid a visit to the 'Church of Jesus' in Setubal, in order to see the splendid example that exists there of Manueline architecture, in particular, those fantastic twisted columns, suggestive of ropes, and reminiscent of the seafaring prowess of the Portuguese, by which that country achieved its greatness. But I couldn't get in. Round and round the church I walked, trying this door and that, but to no avail.

And my text suggests a similar situation. People going round and round the Kingdom of God, trying to get in, but to no avail! Some cry out, 'Lord, Lord,' but the doors don't yield. Others go in for long and elaborate services of devotion, sometimes at real cost to personal comfort, but no way of entry opens up. Others even earn a name for being religious. I can think of a layman in a village I know, who loves to walk around in a cassock, but to look at his face I should find it hard to believe that he had really entered the Kingdom of God.

What is the Kingdom of God? Too many of us discover no meaning in our Lord's words, because so often we count the Kingdom of God as something which only belongs to the future, something on the other side of death, a phrase which might almost be equivalent to heaven. That aspect exists, but what we must remember is that the Kingdom of God exists in the present. It is God's rule of love in the hearts of men.

But how do you get in? The *first* answer is, not through the door of pious phrases. It could, I think, be said that not many people are queueing up outside this door today. The unctuousness Dickens used to love to caricature is out. Perhaps it never did lay hold of members of the Established Church to any marked degree, though it is surprising what can be got away with, provided the conversation be generously sprinkled with words like 'Catholic' and 'sacramental.' And the Evangelicals, for their part, have quite a vocabulary of their own, used as a kind of test of peoples' participation in this form of religion. The repetition of the right phrases, however, should have little weight put on it. It is not by saying, 'Lord, Lord,' or 'It's Catholic, it's Catholic!' or the man is 'keen,' that we gain entry into the Kingdom of God. Words are important, and phrases can be meaningful, but they do not automatically force doors in the life of the Spirit. Jesus said, 'Not everyone that saith unto me, "Lord, Lord," shall enter into the Kingdom of heaven.'

How do you get in? The *second* answer is, not by good works. At first it might appear that in saying this I have distorted the text, or even gone against it in flat contradiction. 'Not everyone that saith unto me, "Lord, Lord," shall enter into the Kingdom of heaven; but he that doeth the will of my Father which is in heaven.' Does not the text teach that not talking, but doing, is the way of entry into the Kingdom of God? Yes, but the doing is 'doing the will of my Father which is in heaven.' It is not the doing of what are commonly called 'good works.' St. Paul sounded the death knell once and for all over good works, as the way of entry, when he wrote, 'And though I bestow all my goods to feed the poor, and though I give my body to be burned, and have not charity, it profiteth me nothing.' It is not that we shouldn't give a helping hand to the Missions to Seamen, and to relief work among lepers, and practical encouragement to those who are trying to help in the matter of housing London's homeless, but if we think that these good works will force open the door into the Kingdom of heaven, we are mistaken. It could lead us into the dark dungeons of pride, or the narrow passage of censoriousness. Do you think there was no almsgiving among the Pharisees? There was plenty of it! But neither almsgiving nor service-giving is the way of entry into the Kingdom of God. If pious language could at one time have been said to be the door some Free Church members kept on trying, pious deeds is certainly the door the Established Church has tried; and neither door yields entry into the Kingdom of God.

What does yield entry? How do you get in? The answer is, doing the will of the Father of Jesus, who is in heaven. This means believing in God, believing that he is a Father, believing that he has a will or purpose for us, his people.

And maybe this is easy to assent to in principle, or in theory, but suppose we tie it up to life. Here is a woman who lives alone, her relatives of her own generation have died, indeed, many of her acquaintance, too. Can she believe in God as a Father, who is working out a purpose of love for her?

Here is a young man about to take up his life's work, and

he develops some serious trouble in his eyes. He has been to Moorfields', of course, but he may never see. Can he believe in God as a Father, working out a purpose of love for his life?

What use in situations like this repeating pious phrases, 'Lord, Lord,' 'Catholic, Catholic,' 'Evangelical, Evangelical.' What use in situations like this writing out a cheque for 'Oxfam,' 'Feed the Minds,' 'Save the Children,' or any other good cause you like to name, right and proper as every one of those good causes is, and worthy of our support.

But you can't get into the Kingdom of God that way, that Kingdom which is the rule of God's love in the hearts of men. The door only yields when we do *our living* in the trust that what is happening is somehow in the providence of God, and is meant for our good. We live here and now in London, S.W.7, in the year 1966, in the Kingdom of God's love and peace and power and effectiveness, being different, and appearing different, by just that very entry.

One of the Canons of Hereford Cathedral, who often helps me on the staff of the College of Preachers, told a group of clergy one day of a woman he used to visit in the Diocese of Southwark, where he worked. She was confined to one room at the top of a tenement block, so crippled she could not even turn the pages of a book, or light a cigarette, though some apparatuses have been devised to help her do this. 'But,' said the Canon, 'when I was down, and everything seemed to be wrong, I could go and visit her, and her very happiness transformed my clouded spirit.'

Some others of us have had the experience of meeting people like that, who have gone through the door, into the Kingdom of God. They are not all cripples, not all deprived. I can think of one or two highly-placed ecclesiastics of whom I personally know this to be true. There are many others. They have no reliance on pious language. They do not boast themselves on the good works they have done, though there are many. They daily believe in God the Father, who has a purpose in their lives. And so they live now in the Kingdom of heaven, than which there surely is no better place that we could be. 'Not every one that saith unto me, "Lord, Lord," shall enter into the Kingdom of heaven; but he that doeth the will of my Father, which is in heaven.'

TRINITY 9

Money

St. Luke 16. 9 (NEB) *'So I say to you, use your worldly wealth to win friends for yourselves, so that when money is a thing of the past you may be received into an eternal home.'*

INTRODUCTION

What would you say is *the most difficult of all the parables Jesus told?* Isn't it the one called 'The Dishonest Bailiff'?

And it is all about money, which is dirty stuff. Money comes close to ruling the world, which is why Jesus called it a rival god. 'You cannot serve God and Mammon.' And yet we cannot do without money.

1. *The parable deals with a fiddle over money*
Probably the bailiff, like many in the East, kept two sets of accounts, one set to show his rich overlord, and the other set to show his tenant. In the tables for the overlord, the tenant would be shown as owing 500 gallons of oil; in the tables for the tenant, the same man would be shown as owing 1,000. The bailiff, of course, took the 1,000 from the tenant, and paid 500 to the overlord. That is, he conducted a 'fiddle.' When the overlord smelt trickery, he asked to see the accounts. It put the bailiff 'in a spot.' All he did, however, was to make the tenant's accounts agree with what he had prepared for the overlord. So both parties were happy. The tenant for a reduction, and the overlord his due. And as the bailiff had 'scratched the back' of the tenant, the tenant would be prepared 'to scratch' the bailiff's, if he lost his job, and provide him shelter.

2. What is the lesson?

Not that the bailiff was not dishonest. Not that Christ doesn't assert that our hands aren't dirty. Nor does he excuse us; and for this reason, that he, the clean Christ, is prepared to grasp us by our dirty hands.

This is the lesson. The day will come when we shall be put out of our stewardship of life. Then the question will be asked, not, did you possess any money? but, what did you do with the money you possessed?

3. What is the moral?

The moral is, we should use our money to help people, so that they are indebted to us in gratitude, friendship and appreciation.

Here we have an *a fortiori* argument. If a dishonest bailiff used the money entrusted to him to win friends, how much more should a Christian, who is not dishonest.

CONCLUSION

Money is dirty stuff. It can never *buy* friendship. It cannot *purchase* spiritual qualities. But money is changed by the use to which it is put. If we use it in God's service, and man's service, out of gratitude for what God has done for us in Christ, we shall be acting very wisely. Christ said so.

TRINITY 10

Recognition

St. Luke 19. 44 '... *thou knewest not the time of thy visitation.*'

INTRODUCTION

Imagine, for a moment, a young man being offered a job. The pay is on the low side. The conditions of work second class. He turns it down. He has been very foolish. A deeper study of the situation would have shown him what bright prospects there were in that post. But he loses his chance.

1. *Jerusalem did not recognize its way of peace*

It saw no prospects in Jesus, nothing but submission to Rome. It did not see that God's will for Jerusalem could be accomplished through submission to Rome. It was bent on war. It did not recognize that there is a proper time for all things. This was the time for quietude. It was what God was saying to Jerusalem through Jesus. But they did not recognize 'the time of their visitation.' That is why Jesus wept over Jerusalem.

2. *Our country today does not recognize its way of prosperity*

The Christian Gospel is concerned with man's response to God, and his response to his fellowmen. But what has this to do with economics? So the Gospel is rejected. The Gospel has, however, a great deal to do with economics. No matter how efficient your machinery is, if the men who operate the machines have the wrong spirit, the machines will not be running for very long. At bottom, the efficient running of a country depends on the quality of the people who work it. If our people were better at heart, we should soon be economically solvent. The loss in modern economy through professional crime, and common dishonesty is crippling. But we do not recognize this truth. God is speaking to us now through our trouble. We do not recognize the time of our visitation. God weeps over us.

3. *Notice that Christ did weep*

There was no curse. No threatening. Instead, there was an heartfelt sigh. This is the reaction of one who loves. Christ loved Jerusalem. 'God so loved the world, that he gave....' We must not forget this. But love does not mean weakness. There is no sentimentality in it. Christ loved Jerusalem, but because it closed its eyes to its visitation, Titus the Roman came and left not 'one stone upon another.'

CONCLUSION

God visits his people in hidden forms. It may be under cover of an illness. It may be through a time of economic depression. The important need is to hear what God is saying, and if necessary to be willing to change the course of life we are following. The enemy of safety is stubbornness.

TRINITY 11

Look up, not down

St. Luke 18. 13 *'God be merciful to me a sinner.'*

INTRODUCTION

I can tell you who these two men are. On the day after the prodigal son returned home, it is he and his elder brother who went to church. The elder brother thinking of how he had never run away from home, and squandered his inheritance, 'stood and prayed thus with himself, "God, I thank thee that I am not as other men are...."' The younger brother, the prodigal, 'smote upon his breast, saying, "God be merciful to me a sinner."'

1. *Where the two men were alike*
They both went to church. They both prayed. They both thought of themselves before God in a personal way. Theirs was a personal religion.

2. *Where the two men were different*
The Pharisee looked down when he prayed, down to the man who fiddled and fornicated, and, of course, he counted himself better than he, which was true. The publican looked up when he prayed, up to God, and in doing so realized his own complete unworthiness. 'God be merciful to me a sinner.'

CONCLUSION

If we make comparisons with others, we church people will become Pharisaic and sink in our pride. If we think of our lives only in comparison with Christ, we shall know how much we need God's mercy and forgiveness. We ought to remember this, when we reach the Confession in the Communion service, and the prayer of Humble Access. 'We are not worthy so much as to gather up the crumbs under thy table.' God be merciful to me a sinner.

TRINITY 12

Hearing and speaking

St. Mark 7. 35 *'He spake plain.'*

INTRODUCTION

The basic trouble with this man was deafness. Because he had never heard correctly, he could not speak correctly. Because he could not speak correctly, people counted him a 'half-wit,' and he was, as we say, 'distinctly sub.' Because of this, he was left out of life, a misfit, an almost useless person. All because he had never heard.

1. *The necessity for hearing the Gospel*

The first necessity in the Christian life is not to be 'the good Samaritan,' but to sit down, and listen to what God has to say, through Christ. 'Faith cometh by hearing' (Rom. 10. 17). There must be preaching, and there must be listening.

2. *God radiates his healing to us through 'means'*

Christ spat, and touched this deaf-mute's tongue. God reaches to us through the sacraments. He knows our needs.

3. *The man was made to hear by Christ*

We need to ask God to enable us to hear. The congregation must pray for opened ears, before the ministry of the word. Grace, not simply intelligence, is the requisite for receiving what God has to give.

4. *When the man could hear, he testified to what Christ had done*
This is preaching. It equals publishing, that is, making known what God has done for us. It is what laymen should do, as well as clergy.

CONCLUSION

Are we taking our work of hearing seriously? Do we pray about hearing? Do we recognize hearing as fundamental?

TRINITY 13

My neighbour

St. Luke 10. 29 *'And who is my neighbour?'*

INTRODUCTION

It was after dark and the rain was tumbling down. In order not to skid I slowed down my car, because at the crossroads ahead I could see a man in the middle of the road, waving a walking-stick. When I drew within three yards of him, and stopped, he was still there, and two or three other cars approaching from different directions had done the same. We had all pulled up because of this man. He was old but upright still. There was something distinguished about his clothes, even in that rain. From his bearing, and the way he waved that stick at us, he could have been a retired general in the army, accustomed to command. But that was long ago. Now he was frail. Perhaps he lived alone in a flat nearby. That could easily be. Perhaps he was going out to get a meal in a restaurant. That would account for his presence there in the roadway after dark on a pouring wet night. He wanted to cross to the other side. But in the middle of the road, seeing the cars coming at him from all angles, he panicked. Fear rooted him to the spot. Cars were all around him. And then I saw this happen. A workman in a navy blue duffle coat stepped off the pavement and crossed to the bewildered old gentleman. Socially, they were poles apart. But I heard the workman say, 'Here, let me give yer an 'and, guvnor.' And the last I saw of them was the two walking away together, the young workman helping the old gentleman to recover from his paralysing terror.

1. *And who is my neighbour?*
It is that fellow Anglican, of course, sitting in the pew next to you. Church people need to be neighbourly to each other. In these days of 'ecumenism' (frightening word) we can, in our eagerness to be brotherly to that other denomination down the street, forget to be brotherly to the people with whom we actually live. Not even clergy are as kind to each other as they ought to be. Charity begins at home. But it must not end there. Why? Because the people at home are not always in need, and nearby need is what makes someone not in our home a neighbour.

In the New Testament way of thinking, a man is presented as a neighbour by his need, and he is accepted as a neighbour by those who do something about it. In the Gospel for today the two leaders who figure in the drama we call 'the good Samaritan' certainly did not live close to one another. One came from Samaria, and the other presumably from Judaea, miles apart. But more than miles apart when it came to race, religion and background. They were poles apart. But they were made neighbours by the predicament into which one fell, and from which the other helped him. What happened, of course, is that the Samaritan traveller did not see the robbed traveller as a Jew, he simply saw him as a man. Jesus made his story begin, 'A certain *man.*'

When it comes to people in trouble, we are to forget all about classifying labels. This man is in the five-figure-income bracket. That woman was the guilty woman in a divorce case. But we are to see people as human beings. We are to go out of our way to treat people simply as men and women.

2. *The way to find neighbours*
To find them even in that unfriendly block of flats, even on that new housing estate where everyone is a stranger. Human

need is the pathway to neighbourliness. As long as there is human need, there need not be loneliness. Only in a society where everybody's wants were supplied, would neighbourliness be really difficult to achieve.

3. *But who is the good Samaritan?*
It could be you. It could be me. We pray such will be the case. But the great 'good Samaritan' is Christ. He comes to you from another country, and sees your need. He does not turn you down, nor pass you by, because you haven't always lived up to what you know to be right. His only concern is that you need assistance for living. That is the deepest lesson of all to learn. When the world was 'down,' God did not pass it by. When you are down and I am down, Christ will not retreat to the other side. When you receive into your hands the sacramental Christ, you are renewing, you are allowing to come to your side one who really cares for you, simply because you are a human being with many deep and secret needs. It was wise for the wounded traveller on the Jerusalem to Jericho road to receive the man who stopped to succour him. You will also be wise to welcome the Christ who comes to succour you and all who need his care today.

TRINITY 14

Men afar off

> St. Luke 17. 12 '... *there met him ten men that were lepers, which stood afar off.*'

INTRODUCTION

There are a great many men and women in their company today. As far as the Church is concerned they stand afar off. I do not mean lepers, but people who feel they are not wanted by the Church. Quite a number of young people in this permissive age are going to feel like that some day, if they do not already. But with some there is a longing to 'come in.' Perhaps more than we realize. What should be our attitude?

1. *It could be the way of Pharisaism*

The Pharisees were not bad men. They were sincerely concerned for the welfare of society and the welfare of their Church. They formed the backbone of their society. They were seriously concerned lest standards of life should be pulled down by thoughtlessly allowing those who did not measure up to those standards to stream in. It was sad about those ten lepers, of course, but then where would the health of the community be if you let lepers loose everywhere? They must be kept at a distance. A pity, of course, but what can be done?

2. *It could be the way of Christ*

First of all we must note that these ten lepers themselves wished to meet with Christ. They knew he would not ostracize. They knew he would heal. It was not a case of permitting unhealed men to mix in with the community. Nor did he ignore the regulation for the safeguarding of the community. He bade the lepers show themselves to the priests. Christ, however, makes contact because in the contact there is cleansing.

CONCLUSION

For the Church to keep people afar off is to admit that it possesses no power to change them. This is true, of course, if Christ is not given his rightful place in the Church. But if those afar off are conscious of the Christ, and not of the Pharisees, looking at them from the Church gate, some of them will be encouraged to draw near, and in the welcome which follows, will be changed. Not that they will all become perfect. Only one of the lepers cleansed returned to give thanks. It is interesting, however, that he was the real outsider among them, a Samaritan. Perhaps those most afar off who draw near and find healing are most grateful. That is certainly what Jesus said of the woman who anointed his feet, to the amazement of Simon the Pharisee. He who is forgiven most loves most. Jesus was not a Pharisee, that is, a separatist, and the Church should follow the Lord it professes to serve.

TRINITY 15

Anxiety

St. Matthew 6. 25, 26, 28 *'Therefore I bid you put away anxious thoughts. . . . Look at the birds, . . . Consider the lilies.'*

It does *not* help to look at the birds, or to consider the lilies. It certainly does not rub away anxiety. A man only needs to look at a bed of dahlias the night after a frost has been at work to see why. Or let him walk along the hedgerows when the temperature has remained below 20° F. for three days, and see what has happened to a great many birds. What sense, then, is there in Jesus' words, 'Do not be anxious, look at the birds, consider the lilies . . .'?

But Jesus knew about sparrows falling to the ground. He said so. And he knew that not all seeds bring forth grain. He was, however, thinking of nature in general, thinking of its rhythmic decay and regrowth, thinking of how every part has its function in the purposeful whole by which the splendour is produced. What he said was, if God has a purpose for every bird, flower and the grass of the field, which have such a short life, *how much more* must he have a purpose for human beings who stand outside that structure of the natural order. So he adds, 'You are worth more than birds.'

But still, you say, the verse doesn't help. It is not possible for us to live from day to day like birds and flowers. Quite so. That is Jesus' point. If the birds and flowers can have peace of mind when they cannot work and plan for the future, *how much more* ought you who are able to plan.

A query still, however, remains. What about the people who do work and plan for the future, but lose their jobs through no fault of their own? But Jesus was thinking of man in general. Most men can provide. And if we remind him of the exceptions he will reply, 'Yes, but if the birds and flowers are provided for, who have no organization to help them, *how much more* ought you to see to it that your communal life is so organized that these unfortunates do not suffer over that for which they are not responsible.'

There is, however, one thing we should be anxious about, and that is our ability to stand in the presence of God. 'Set your mind on God's kingdom and his justice before everything else, and all the rest will come to you as well.' That is what Jesus said.

We can see this work out at the purely human level. Here is a man asking a girl to marry him. What does she answer? If she says, 'Alright, but what sort of car shall we have if I do, a Mini or a Jaguar?' What sort of married life will follow a marriage on that basis of primary interest in things? Would it not be all cares, all worry, all fretfulness and endless anxiety? But see the girl who marries because of the man's character which she loves with all her heart, does she care if she starts with a Mini, or no Mini at all? Their love makes those things a matter of indifference, but what you find in practice is that the couple come to possess enough of those things to fulfil themselves in life and love.

Jesus said, 'Set your minds on God's kingdom . . . and all the rest will come.' And if, like the present preacher, our eyes have been opened to appreciate this text by Bultmann's exposition of it in *Marburger Predigten* (pages 14 f.), it is our Lord's words that will strengthen us when we see how they are built up on an *a fortiori* argument. If God has a purpose for the birds and flowers, *how much more* has he a purpose in his providence for you who are worth more than they. Do not be anxious.

TRINITY 16

The barrier of bereavement

St. Luke 7. 13 (NEB) *'When the Lord saw her his heart went out to her.'*

INTRODUCTION

She was moving as in a trance. No sights nor sounds nor smells penetrated the curtains of her consciousness as she proceeded to the cemetery. The accompanying crowd might not have been there. All around her hung the barrier of her bereavement, isolating her to everything, except the fact that once she had lost her husband, and now she had lost her son. A defenceless woman, alone in the world.

1. *Barriers*

In chapter seven of his sensitive Gospel, St. Luke sets this widow of Nain along with three others as instances of people standing on the other side of a barrier. A centurion living behind a high wall of racial difference, aware of his remoteness. John the Baptist walled up in the prison of his doubts. A nameless woman on the other side of the moral partition which ran through the midst of respectable society. This widow of Nain was the second in this series of four barred-off people. It is Luke only who tells her story.

2. *Sorrow*

This woman's isolating barrier was her sorrow. Sorrow can isolate. Bereavement can isolate. Even friends can be known to shun the society of the bereaved. Awkward with sadness, clumsy with sorrow, they turn their steps away. The withdrawal of friends, however, is not that which constitutes the isolation. It is the numbing, unbelievable, unaccepted (as yet) consciousness that a person loved is beyond the reach of human sight or touch. No hope stirred in this woman's heart, no faith reached out to Jesus, she made no appeal. There is no evidence that she was even aware of his existence.

3. Compassion

But he watched her. And his heart went out to her. That is the Gospel for the sixteenth Sunday after Trinity. Just that. The Lord (St. Luke uses that title) was moved by the sight of a woman in tears behind a separating wall of heartbreaking sorrow. And he crossed that wall for no other reason than compassion, just as he crossed it for the three other cases described in chapter seven of St. Luke.

CONCLUSION

The Lord does not always give back loved ones, even from the jaws of death, though sometimes this does happen. But he stands by, and is watching. What is more significant, his heart goes out and through the isolating wall of sorrow. There is nothing else that can penetrate this barrier, but compassion. Christ has it. God has it. It reaches out to all, long before they even ask or think of it. *This is the lesson*, love only will break through the isolating barrier of bereavement. If we are wise, we shall let that restoring love reach out and through to us when we stand, as some day we shall, in the company of this woman, there behind her separating wall.

TRINITY 17

Exclusiveness excluded

1. *Healing on the Sabbath*

The opening words of the Gospel today are arresting because they tell us about Jesus entering a house on the Sabbath day to eat bread. That is what we are here to do. But in this story the hosts had unworthy motives. (That is possible even at the Eucharist.) They kept an eye open to see what Jesus would do about a man suffering from dropsy. Perhaps they had 'planted' him there on purpose. Perhaps the whole incident was 'rigged,' as we say. They wanted to catch him out with healing on the Sabbath day. And, of course, they did. Jesus healed the man. What is more, he justified his action by an appeal to common sense. You would pull out an ass or an ox that had fallen into a pit on the Sabbath day, wouldn't you? We must notice this. In his approach to the religious life, Jesus appealed to reason. And reason cried aloud for a break with exclusive traditions. Was this ill man to be shut out from the healing power of God because it was the Sabbath day?

2. *Order of precedence*

But there was more to come. Before the meal began there was an unattractive scramble for chief seats. Everybody wanted the exclusive seats at the top of the table. Then Jesus told his parable. It must have created quite a scene when uttered in the presence of those pushing past to get close to the V.I.P.s. He told them to go and sit in the humblest seats, and then, if they were worthy, they would be called up higher.

3. *Exclusiveness*

That is the trouble. Exclusiveness seems to be in our blood. No matter what reason and human needs demand, we can fall into the trap of being governed simply by what has always been done in the past. Traditions can become excluding agencies. So the needs of persons get disregarded. And people can set their hearts on nothing so much as belonging to an exclusive set. It is true, there have to be people 'at the top,' but position must be awarded for merit, and not sought for the sake of exclusiveness. Exclusiveness should play no part in the life of a Christian. He is where he is not simply because of his own merit. The Christian must be open to all, as Christ was open to all, and God is open to all, and certainly no tradition must ever stop him from helping a person in need. Reason is against it, and any religious faith which has reason against it stands under the judgement of Christ.

TRINITY 18

A sharp tongue

1. *The ability to silence people*
Here is action on the part of Jesus we should like to copy. But ought we to? Certainly not unless we understand it. It is the ability to silence people with devastating repartee. This is *what today's Gospel is about.* The opening verse tells us he put the Sadducees to silence, and the closing verses tell us how he floored the Pharisees and curbed the will of any of his critics to attempt to trap him with clever words. Jesus was always that bit more clever.

2. *We would like to be able to wield our own tongues powerfully, like that*
Some people spend their lives cultivating the skill. But the motive behind such action is personal pride. We fancy ourselves as conquerors of our fellows, and do not trouble about the wounds we may have inflicted. The tongue can be a most offensive instrument. St. James, in his Epistle, warns us about the use of the tongue.

3. *When did Jesus use this skill of powerful, thrusting language?*
Study the Gospels, and you will see that for him it was a defensive weapon only, and not an offensive one. He used this skill only when he was hemmed in by his enemies. And the promise is made that in their times of testing and trial, Christians will be given this same gift of the right words to utter, when the time of need arises. 'I will give you a mouth of wisdom, which all your adversaries shall not be able to withstand or to gainsay' (Lk. 21. 15). Peter and John experienced this when hauled before their rulers in order to explain how they had healed a man at the gate of the Temple (Acts 4. 8 f.).

4. *A gift of the spirit*
What we have to remember is that this gift of telling speech, what St. Paul calls 'a word of wisdom' (1 Cor. 12. 8), is not a

human accomplishment, but a gift of the divine spirit; and no gifts of the divine spirit are for personal aggrandisement, but only for the building up of the Christian congregation. Moreover, all gifts must be subordinated to the exercise of Christian love.

CONCLUSION

We Christians must never seek to acquire or fall into the trap of developing a biting tongue. If we are in a tight corner for our faith, as our master was, it may be that we shall be given the right words to speak, and deliverance may be the result. But brilliant speech saved neither Jesus nor Stephen. Don't set too great a store by clever talking. That is where the members of the Church at Corinth went wrong, and St. Paul had to correct them. 'Though I speak with the tongues of men and of angels,' he said, '... it profiteth me nothing.'

TRINITY 19

A passenger

1. *Not his fault*

It wasn't this man's fault that he was a passenger in life, and his friend had to carry him along. He had palsy, or paralysis, or 'polio.' The first fact to notice, however, is that he was a passenger.

There are people in the community, sometimes even in church or in their homes, who are passengers. They contribute almost nothing, they expect everything to be done for them; they are, of course, indescribably dull. Perhaps it isn't always their fault. Perhaps they lack ideas. Perhaps life only pumps feebly through their bodies and their minds. They are 'weaker brethren,' and Christian people must always be ready to carry them. It is doubtful if we ought to carry passengers on our committees, but we must certainly be prepared to carry them in life. They test the depth of our understanding and self-control.

2. *Probably his fault*

It looks as if this man's paralysis in today's Gospel was his own fault. This is not always, perhaps not often, the case, but it seems possible here, or why did Jesus begin, 'Son, be of good cheer, thy sins be forgiven thee.' Perhaps the man was regretting the life he had lived. Perhaps he reckoned it was too late for him to expect a chance now. So he was depressed, and his depression was increasing his paralysis. 'Mind' affects body.

It is possible some of the passengers in the community, church and home need not be passengers at all. It is their fault. They have never really laid hold on what the Christian faith offers us. It offers us the knowledge that God has a purpose for each one of us, however different we may be from our neighbours. At the Lord's table the words are specific and individual, 'The body of our Lord Jesus Christ which was given for *thee*, preserve *thy* body and soul unto eternal life.' It is for each one of us to believe God, and to rise up to the call which comes in Christ. Today at the Eucharist Christ says to every communicant, 'Arise and walk.' Make your contribution to the life around you, and do not be carried again.

3. *Christ came to deal with faults*

In Capernaum they marvelled when they saw this paralytic walking and carrying his mattress. That is what men's reaction should be to what they see going on in the churches—'passengers' being turned into contributing citizens. It can happen when we believe the Gospel the Eucharist proclaims. Do we believe it? Have we really thought how the Christ is looking at us today, and calling, 'Thy sins be forgiven thee. Arise and walk.' Don't be a passenger any more, stand up on your feet. Make your contribution to life now.'

TRINITY 20
Not bothering

1. *It is the man who attended the wedding feast without a wedding garment who sticks in our minds*
Don't try to excuse him. He did not try to excuse himself. When he was questioned, he was speechless. He didn't say he was too poor, or that he hadn't time to change. The probability is that he was one of the original guests who were invited to dinner, but when he saw that all the riff-raff of the locality were invited to make up for those 'top people' who couldn't come, he didn't bother to change. It couldn't be much of a party, anyway, with all that lot coming! He'd turn up, but he wasn't going to wear his best clothes for a 'show like that.' That was his sin, thinking lightly of the king's provision because of the other people who attended. He got turned out for that superiority of his.

2. *Some people adopt a superior attitude*
There is always a danger that people will look down on the Gospel, and the sacramental representation of it, because of those who present themselves to receive it—'not many mighty, not many noble.' There are those who adopt a superior attitude to Christ because of the Church. The German philosopher Nietzsche was not the only one. It is very dangerous to fix one's gaze critically at the congregation, and not gratefully on Christ.

3. *The necessity for proper preparation*
This man should have taken trouble when he came to the king's feast. We should take trouble when we come to the *Lord's table*. It is easy not to bother, easy not to discipline our minds, easy not to repent of our sins before we come, easy just to 'roll up anyhow.' To do so is to incur the probability of the Lord's wrath. The proper preparation is to clothe ourselves with the garments of penitence, humility and gratitude for being allowed to come. And above all, to fix our eyes on the Cross and what the Christ has done to make this feast possible.

No darkness, binding and weeping will follow this kind of attendance, but freedom, joy and new strength, a real Eucharist, a real thanksgiving—if we wear the proper clothes.

TRINITY 21
Thy son liveth

1. Life comes through the word of Jesus
Three times, like a refrain in a symphony, the words, 'Thy son liveth' sound forth. They declare the message. Life comes through the word of Jesus. He simply speaks. Neither physical proximity nor physical contact is necessary. From a distance, even beyond the range of sight, Jesus speaks, and life is the result. The words become events. All this is an indication of what preaching should be, the production of life by means of words.

2. The beneficiary
He appeared to lack the obvious qualifications for receiving favours. That he was a noble man, a king's man or courtier attached to Herod Antipas' court, indicates that he was probably a Gentile, perhaps the Roman centurion described in St. Matthew's Gospel. Thus, he was an outsider to Israel. And the event took place in Galilee, not Judea and Jerusalem, where men should have been sympathetic to Jesus but were not. This story is linked to that of the wedding feast in Cana, because both described incidents in territory outside the heart of Judaism proper. But the point is, this kingsman had faith, and because of it, three times the refrain beats out, 'Thy son liveth.' Life is possible anywhere, and among any people, however outside established religion they may appear to be.

3. A parable about faith
The story of this man's faith is to be understood, however, as *a parable*, an analogy, or as a sign of what the true faith is. It is not the true faith itself. What we see in this story is a man

driven by desperation to ask for a miracle. Jesus grants it. But in doing so he asserts that faith which is sustained by such wonders is not the highest type of faith. Disparagingly he says, 'Except ye see signs and wonders, ye will not believe.' But the nobleman's faith is a pointer to the true faith. The true faith is complete trust in Christ alone without reliance on our own status or merit, but it is also faith which does not need to be nourished by signs or wonders. It is trust in the word.

CONCLUSION

Life in the spirit, eternal life is the possession of the Church, not because of its history, its pedigree or its accomplishments, but because when everything seems against it, it still trusts implicitly in Christ and his word. Then it lives. Its members live with it. They will, in fact, never die.

TRINITY 22

Ethics

INTRODUCTION

How ought the servant in this story to have treated his fellow-servant who owed him, as the New English Bible says, only a few pounds? We are told that he 'laid hands on him,' 'took him by the throat' and brutally demanded, 'pay me that thou owest.' Is this the way to approach a debtor, showing no mercy, in spite of pleas for mercy, but casting the offender into prison? How should we treat those who have wronged us?

1. *Harshness is one way*

In today's parable, this way caused sorrow among the members of the community, that one of their number should have so acted, and anger on the part of the master. He even made his servant suffer for his harsh attitude. We gather God is involved in the results that accrue from harsh human behaviour.

2. Worldly wisdom is another way

It is better not to treat the underdog harshly, because, who knows? he may be the top dog some day, and then where are you? Eighteenth-century France and nineteenth-century Russia might at least have thought of this. Perhaps parts of Africa ought to be thinking of it today.

3. Sentimental leniency is a third way

Too often this stems from a sense of bad conscience. We know our own thoughts and acts would not stand up to a public inquiry. So we excuse all faults in the hope that our own would be excused. What is being thought of in this case, is the judgement of man. Leniency, however, does not arrest the rot of wrong doing.

CONCLUSION

How we should treat those who have wronged us is answered in this parable, not by side looks to our fellowmen's judgement, but by the upward look to God. How I should treat my neighbour is conditioned by how God treats me. God is not lenient. He does not say debts do not matter. He demands payment. Sin is labelled for what it is, and reparation must be made. God is a God of standards, a God who demands right living. He will, however, forgive if we ask, not for our rights, but for his mercy. This is not easy, because of the implications, but it works. We are not crushed. We are lifted up to try once more. And here is the answer to our question. We are to treat our fellowmen in the way God treats us.

Ethics, then, are based on the Gospel. Because God has forgiven me my debt to him in terms of sins (often called debts), I can never hope to pay, I must forgive my fellowman the wrong he has done me *if he asks*. This qualifies the phrase sometimes heard, 'I can never forgive him for that.' But what if he comes and asks, even kneels down and asks for mercy. What then? Peter 'caved in' and agreed that in such a case he would forgive up to seven times, but that was the limit. Jesus said we should put no limit on our forgiveness in such cases. And the reason is because God puts no limit on his forgiveness of us when we confess our wrongs. How we should treat our neighbours should be governed by what we know of the way God treats us. Ethics rest on the Gospel of God's forgiveness.

TRINITY 23
The sacred and the secular

1. *A trap*

Before it became a trap for Christians, it was laid as a trap for Christ. But it did not catch him. The trap concerns the relation of the sacred to the secular. For Jesus it was made to take this form, 'Are we or are we not permitted to pay taxes to the Roman Emperor?' If he said 'Yes,' he was caught. He would forfeit the support of the Jews. If he said 'No,' he was also caught. He would bring down upon himself the charge of being a rebel to Rome. But he was not caught. He replied, 'Pay Caesar what is due to Caesar, and pay God what is due to God.'

2. *Twofold obligation*

Christians have been caught when they have imagined that there are two independent and unrelated spheres of life, the sacred and the secular. In practice this has meant that some have tried to keep their hands off what they call political questions. And so abuses have been allowed to develop in the community without one word of protest from the churches. Because, however, a man has a body living under temporal conditions, he is subject to earthly concerns. He cannot contract out. Because he is a living soul he is also subject to an heavenly kingdom to which, as a Christian, he freely gives his allegiance. In both these spheres the Christian must fulfil his obligations. 'Pay Caesar what is due to Caesar, and pay God what is due to God.' There may be times when the Christian has to choose between God and Caesar, between the sacred and the secular. This is when Caesar, or the secular assumes divine prerogative. But so long as the civil government performs its functions of providing the condition in which a man can fulfil himself as a citizen, it is entitled to its taxes.

3. *Danger of quietism*
Christians, therefore, are law-abiding citizens, as Christ was. He paid the tax due from him. But Christians are caught in a trap if they think they must be quietist. This is exactly what their enemies want. They want ineffective Christians. And that is what Christians become if they do not grasp the relations between the sacred and the secular.

TRINITY 24

Disease and death

1. *Disease and Death: the two enemies of life*
Normally the one follows the other in a dismal procession. But in today's Gospel we are shown the Lord of life halting the procession, and making it return the way it had come. This is not the work of a living man, but the work of Life Incarnate. From his presence disease and death retreat like bacteria from penicillin.

2. *The Life-giver is, however, the Lord*
We cannot manipulate him to make him do our will. The healing he provides is always his gift. We cannot make a gift come, otherwise it is no gift. We must remember this in regard to faith. The faith of the ruler whose daughter was dead did not *make* the Lord's life-giving power come to her. The woman who had a haemorrhage did not cause the healing power to flow into her because she exercised faith. What faith does is to make possible the reception. Faith is the hand outstretched for what may be given.

3. *The cause of the cure*
We notice in the case of the woman that she was cured by

touching the *clothes of Jesus*. This is not a case of primitive magic, nor the relic of primitive magical ideas. What healed was Christ's real presence. The clothes she touched were *his* clothes. They were the symbol of him. Similarly, in the book of the Acts of the Apostles, we read of the shadow of Peter being sought, and items of clothing being taken from Paul. This was because these things were the symbols of the presence of the Apostles, 'the sent ones' of Christ. What we have here is healing power, flowing through symbols, Christ's healing through Christ's symbols.

CONCLUSION

On the Holy table today are set the symbols or sacraments of Christ's real presence. It is not the symbols which can give life and healing. There is no magic in the Christian religion. But through contact with this we may have contact with the Christ, whose gift life and healing is. But like the ruler seeking on behalf of his daughter, and the woman seeking on behalf of herself, we must come with faith, or we have no hands with which to receive. And we must remember, Christ is the Lord. We cannot make him do what we want; we know, however, how full he is of compassion and mercy. The wise course is to seek his presence, to seek him now, to seek him in this service, to come and touch his garment....

TRINITY 25

Nothing lost

> St. John 6. 12 '*Gather up the fragments that remain, that nothing be lost.*'

INTRODUCTION

Unless you can read Greek, you cannot know how appropriate is the scripture passage for today's Gospel for this service. But the words translated, 'when he had given thanks,' that is, after Jesus had taken the loaves, are represented by one Greek

word, *eucharistesas*, which anyone can at once recognize as
'Eucharist.' What can we learn about our Eucharist from this
scripture?

1. *Human resources and human provision are useless to meet the
   needs of men*

Philip showed this by reckoning up the cost of feeding the
crowd that had assembled. Andrew showed it by indicating
the paucity of the provisions among them. This is a humili-
ating lesson, because we are so proud of our achievements,
especially in our technological era. But not even our religion,
nothing we bring is adequate to provide lasting satisfaction.
Neither ritual nor music suffice.

2. *Man can only be given life-giving food by God*

Remember, the five barley loaves and the two small fishes
were God's. They were his creation, though they were in the
possession of the lad. When, therefore, Jesus took them, he
was taking his own. It was God doing with his creation what
man can never do with it. This is the lesson. We cannot make
the wafer bread on the Lord's table today do very much.
We cannot make the wine effective. But God can do with
his own what we can never make it do. He can feed us with
himself. He can feed us unto life eternal.

3. *Nothing must be, nothing can be, lost which God provides*

When the five thousand had eaten, Jesus told the disciples to
'Gather up the fragments that remain, that nothing be lost.'
This is why the remains of the elements left at a communion
service are reverently consumed. We cannot waste what God
gives. God does not let it be wasted. God does not waste his
people. They are not lost unto eternity. What he has taken,
blessed and used, he will preserve. So the Eucharist has a
reference beyond meeting our needs for this life. Listen to the
words carefully, 'The body of our Lord Jesus Christ, which
was given for thee, preserve thy body and soul unto everlasting
life.'

CONCLUSION

This is the last Sunday in the Church's year. God has touched our lives in many ways. We should know that none of those experiences, some of them breaking experiences, will be lost. Nothing God touches is wasted. It will be turned to some eternal purpose, beyond what we at present can see. 'Gather up the fragments that remain, that nothing be lost.'